S0-AFN-902

46 PAGES

Thomas Paine, COMMON SENSE,
and the Turning Point
to Independence

by Scott Liell

MJF BOOKS
NEW YORK

Published by MJF Books
Fine Communications
322 Eighth Avenue
New York, NY 10001

46 Pages
LC Control Number 2006924744
ISBN-13: 978-1-56731-781-7
ISBN-10: 1-56731-781-2

Copyright © 2003 by Scott Liell

This edition published by MJF Books in arrangement with Running
Press Book Publishers, A Member of the Perseus Books Group.

Jacket: John Trumbull, The Death of General Warren at the Battle of
Bunker's Hill, 17 June 1775, detail, Yale University Art Gallery,
Trumbull Collection.

Jacket adapted from original design by Whitney Cookman
Interior designed by Serrin Bodmer
Edited by Joelle Herr and Jeanine Rosen

All rights reserved. No part of this publication may be reproduced or
transmitted in any form or by any means, electronic or mechanical,
including photocopy, recording, or any information storage and
retrieval system, without the prior written permission of the publisher.

Printed in the United States of America.

MJF Books and the MJF colophon are trademarks of
Fine Creative Media, Inc.

QM   10 9   8   7   6   5   4   3   2   1

❧ For my wife, Abigail ❧

CONTENTS

ACKNOWLEDGMENTS

A ny book covering the subject I have chosen to write about must begin by acknowledging the many gifted and dedicated scholars who make such an inquiry as this possible. In that regard, I would like to thank Bernard Bailyn, whose work on the ideological aspects of the revolutionary period has been an indispensable asset. I must also thank the authors of the Paine biographies that I leaned upon heavily—Eric Foner, David Freeman Hawke, and Jack Fruchtman, Jr. Most of all, I extend my gratitude to the dedicated folks in the Franklin Library at Yale University, and indeed to the entire research staff at Yale's Sterling Memorial Library.

Carlo DeVito at Running Press was present at the very conception of this project, and his wisdom, experience, and passion were a constant support throughout. Joelle Herr and Katie Greczylo also added their own care and expertise at important junctures during the process. Whatever I have succeeded in creating between these covers would have been a far poorer piece without the sum total of their generous contributions.

Finally, and foremost, I thank my wife and our two children for their patient sufferance of my chronic absence and absent-mindedness during the research and writing of this book.

"I know not whether any man in the world has had more influence on its inhabitants or affairs for the last thirty years than Tom Paine."

—John Adams

"The mind once enlightened cannot again become dark."

—Thomas Paine

A DECLARATION OF DEPENDENCE

I t had already been an unbearably hot summer, and the first week of July brought no relief. On the floor of the Philadelphia State House the delegates to the second Continental Congress were engaged in an equally heated debate on the subject of a declaration they were in the process of creating. The unfinished declaration was far from universally endorsed by the congressional delegates. There were significant differences as to exactly what to declare, what to demand, and what to threaten should those demands not be met. They were, however, agreed almost to a man about one important point. What the Congress as a whole would not contemplate—what they did not dare to declare, demand, or threaten—was *independence*.

The year was 1775, and the document the delegates would ultimately agree to on July 6 was the Declaration of the Causes and Necessity of Taking up Arms. The purpose of this declaration was to justify before the world their armed resistance to the British Parliament's attempt to enforce an absolute authority over the colonies. Close upon the heels of that primary objective, the document also showed a desire to define the limits of that resistance. The entire enterprise had been undertaken over the objections of a small but vocal minority in Congress, men such as John Adams who insisted that the time for such grovelling gestures had long since passed. But the climate in the colonies in the summer of 1775 was not right for such men or such ideas. The conciliatory declaration of July 6 was ultimately signed by all delegates, even Adams, as was a similarly styled petition directly to George III ratified and signed two days later on July 8, 1775. This second document has come to be called the Olive Branch Petition, and that is what it truly was. Together, these documents represented a sincere if optimistic attempt by the second Continental Congress to lay out their grievances, describe the conditions that would have to precede the ultimate reconciliation they all expected and desired, and assure the crown of the still-strong bonds of affection and loyalty that would surely outlast these momentary quarrels. With an invocation of the "impartial Judge and Ruler of the Universe," the declaration closed:

> . . . we most devoutly implore his divine goodness to protect us happily through this great conflict, to dispose our adversaries to reconciliation on reasonable terms, and thereby to relieve the empire from the calamities of civil war.

In many ways these two documents offer an accurate snapshot of the second Continental Congress, and indeed of the colonial mood in general, one year before the Declaration of Independence. They reveal a people who increasingly believed that their way of life was under attack and that their traditional liberties were being eroded. At the same time, they felt that English law was on their side and even appealed to "their" constitution, the English constitution, to support that claim. The colonials saw the Parliament and the king's ministers as their enemies, not George III himself. And they believed that, if conflict could not be avoided, it would be a civil war between disaffected segments of the British Empire, not a war for independence. For all their anger and perceived ill treatment, they saw themselves as British citizens living abroad, not as American citizens struggling against a foreign oppressor.

How is it, then, that one year later that same Congress, composed of most of the same delegates and representing the same colonies, could find itself so utterly changed? How is it that such recent affinity for Great Britain and her "best of Kings" could give way to the determined—and more famous—declaration "that these united colonies are and of right ought to be free and independent states" and "that they are absolved from all allegiance to the British Crown"? In a relative blink of an eye the spirit of reconciliation would modulate into a passion for independence. In Congress, the marginalized pro-independence minority, or independents led by the Massachusetts and Virginia delegations, would find themselves riding a wave of public support that would carry them to the front ranks of influence and power. The people of the American colonies who had felt so keenly their blood ties to their English compatriots would become prepared to see that blood spilled and commingled on battlefields stretching from Montreal to Savannah. A familial squabble would explode into a full-blown war between two separate nations each willing to court military, economic, and political disaster to make the other submit. But how would it happen? Why? When?

On January 10, 1776, bookstalls in Philadelphia began to sell the first printing of a new pamphlet entitled simply *Common Sense*. The small work publicly set forth for the first time a diverse pro-independence credo that until then had only been whispered privately. It also opened a compelling new line of argument that went far beyond anything advocated by even the most ardent *inde-*

pendent. Typeset and distributed by Robert Bell from his print shop on Third Street, its author went unnamed, identifying himself only as "an Englishman." In spite of a steep two-shilling cover price, the pamphlet was an immediate runaway hit, going on to sell 120,000 copies in its first three months. In a country of less than three million people this was, and remains, an unprecedented success. Even so, the number sold was probably still far below the true audience reached by *Common Sense.* As its reputation and popularity spread, individual copies were read and re-read to countless assembled groups in public houses, churches, army camps, and private parlors throughout the colonies.

The author of this early American bestseller, a bold new statement of the case for independence, was variously thought to be one of the local Philadelphia *intelligentsia* such as Benjamin Franklin or Benjamin Rush, or one of those infamous pro-independence firebrands from Boston, Samuel or John Adams. He was neither. Nor was he a member of Congress at all. Nor was he even an American.

Thomas Paine arrived in the colonies from England a mere fourteen months before the publication of *Common Sense.* Besides two letters of recommendation from Benjamin Franklin, whose acquaintance he had made in London, he came to Philadelphia carrying little in the way of money, reputation, or prospects. What he did possess—to a degree that even Franklin might have blushed at—was a passionate attachment to liberty in all its forms and an abiding hatred of tyranny, especially in its English form.

It was these two qualities—his belief in liberty and his abhorrence of tyranny—that would mark all of Paine's major work, winning him admirers and enemies from Philadelphia to London to Paris. It was also these two qualities, and the forceful, direct way in which Paine expressed them, that made *Common Sense* the single most influential political work in American history, rivaled perhaps only by the *Communist Manifesto* in the history of the world.

There were, of course, other events that contributed to the mounting anger and resentment that culminated in the Declaration of Independence, but *Common Sense* was the critical pivot. The king's contemptuous dismissal of the Olive Branch Petition, Virginia's Royal Governor inciting a slave revolt, rumors of an armada of foreign mercenaries sent by the king to crush the rebellion, and the burning of Norfolk, Virginia, and Falmouth, Maine, all added to the escalation of ill will in the first half of 1776. Similar outrages and provocations, though, had been occurring sporadically since the relationship between England and her colonies first began to deteriorate in 1763. They had provoked angry, sometimes violent, responses from the colonists, but, in each case, the disaffection only went so deep. The long-term effect was minimal, and the colonists' fundamental faith in the ultimate felicity of the British Commonwealth remained intact. This makes it all the more remarkable that, within the space of a few short months during the winter and spring of 1776, *Common Sense* accomplished what even the bloodshed at Lexington and Concord could not—a wholesale annihilation of the emotional and intellectual ties that bound the American colonists to the British crown and country.

One of the main obstacles to the colonies pursuing a path that would end in independence was their political, cultural, and economic fragmentation. Paine recognized that in order to become free the colonies would first need to be united. Since he had very little acquaintance with the country outside Philadelphia, Paine, of necessity, largely ignored these regional divisions and distinctions. Instead, he pursued his argument with a ruthless economy, tracing almost every evil in colonial society back to what he saw as the root evil of British rule. In the same way, he argued that almost every benefit to which the colonists might aspire could be achieved only by casting out the British tyrants. By combining the colonists' diverse grievances into a single grievance and all potential policies into a single policy, he convinced his geographically dispersed readers that their interests were one and the same. Whatever their parochial concerns, Paine suggested, they must all embrace a common objective— American independence. Seen in this light, the interest of New York was the interest of Pennsylvania. The fate of New England fishermen was inextricably intertwined with the fate of southern planters. The British had always relied upon the colonies' different, sometimes competing, cultural, political, and economic interests to keep them fragmented, but these divisions receded as the colonies read and adopted what John Adams called the new "common faith" put forth in *Common Sense*.

In addition to addressing the practical, economic, and political obstacles standing in the way of independence, Paine showed an uncanny sensitivity to the less tangible but even more intractable modes of thought that kept the average colonist from embracing the idea of independence. As a direct frontal assault on the reconciliation mindset and its basic assumptions, *Common Sense* was devastatingly successful. Its author systematically laid waste to the architecture of tradition, habit, and plain old superstition that gave substance to the mythology of America's dependence upon Great Britain.

When Patrick Henry demanded before the Virginia convention in 1775, "Give me Liberty or give me Death," his passion was compelling, but his speech was less radical than it seemed on the face of it. What he demanded—and what the vast majority of colonists at that time wanted—was not liberty *from* but liberty *within* the British Empire. The political vision that animated their words and their actions was actually quite a conservative one. They sought a return to an idealized, more pure version of the constitutional monarchy that they felt had existed before the encroachments of a corrupt parliament and the king's rapacious ministers. The idea of following their fortunes outside of British guidance and protection was frightening and unimaginable to most colonists. Paine appealed to this native conservatism by arguing that the entire British system of government was itself a dangerous, illegitimate innovation, corrupting rather than preserving what was in fact man's natural state of liberty.

Paine, the Englishman, knew better than most the power of the king as a symbol and of the "Ancient Prejudices" that perpetuated that symbolism. He recognized that as long as the people retained their affection for and belief in the British crown, every oppressive measure emanating from England, no matter how odious, would be taken as the work of Parliament, colonial ministers, or royal advisors. Therefore, from the opening pages of his pamphlet, Paine launched a withering attack on the idea of monarchy in general and of the British crown in particular.

One by one, Paine isolated and attacked the individual strands of habituated thought that, woven together, formed the enduring bond between king and subject. He assaulted the almost divine aura of mystery and awe that protected kings from reproach or accountability by pointing out that the "paltry rascally origin" of English kings was a "French bastard landing with an armed banditti," referring to William the Conqueror. He turned a cold Age-of-Enlightenment gaze upon the practice of hereditary rule and suggested that "how a race of men came into the world so exalted above the rest, and distinguished like some new species, is worth inquiring into" to discover "whether they are a happiness or a misery to mankind." But Paine reserved his sharpest quills and most rabid prose for what was probably the most deeply embedded, yet subtly powerful of assumptions—the idea of George III as the father and the colonists as children within his extended family. Paine knew instinctively that this *family romance* had to be utterly exploded before the colonists could embrace the possibility of severing ties with the empire. As long as it endured, this potent metaphor would stand as an ancient rebuke against any "child" so disloyal as to take sides against their "parent," whatever their complaints. *Common*

Sense subtly alternated between undermining the king-as-father concept and using it to make George III's repeated offenses seem all the more cruel and unnatural: "Even brutes do not devour their young, nor savages make war upon their own families."

The suppressed rage that animated Paine's writing in *Common Sense* was another important factor in its success. War with England would have entailed great sacrifice and danger for Americans, and the dry, legalistic arguments put forth by previous polemicists had been insufficient to incite the people to take that fateful step. Where earlier pamphlets recounted a litany of unconstitutional transgressions, Paine felt, and made his readers feel, "wounds of deadly hate." *Common Sense* did not merely change minds, it inflamed passions. This rage originated in Paine's own bitterness toward the English system in which he was reared, and it required a unique style of political writing—one that allowed an author to give vent to those passions more fully than ever before.

What set his writing apart from that of other capable participants in the political arena of the day was that Paine wrote in the language of the public house, while they wrote in the language of the courthouse. He argued not as an advocate before the bar, but as a street corner radical. Most American political pamphleteers wrote to be read and discussed by their peers. Paine wrote first and foremost to be heard and understood by a mass audience. By writing in an accessible, demotic style, Paine invited all Americans into a debate that had been previously confined for the most part to an educated, politically active few. He constructed his arguments from materials that were familiar to the average colonist, favoring allusions to popular history, nature, and scripture rather than Montesquieu, Tacitus, and Cicero. By including all of the colonists in the discussion that would determine their future, *Common Sense* became not just a critical step in the journey toward American independence but also an important artifact in the foundation of American democracy.

As the ideas contained in *Common Sense* gained currency in villages, towns, and parishes throughout the colonies, a groundswell of pro-independence sentiment soon rebounded upon the elected representatives in the Continental Congress. Delegates that had been deliberately instructed by their constituents to vote against independence were told to vote for it. Other delegates, sent to Philadelphia from pro-independence colonies, found themselves answering charges of inaction and hesitancy. In the span of a few short months, the impact of *Common Sense* traveled full circle. From a small print shop on Third Street, it had moved out across the American countryside like a brushfire in dry season and returned with redoubled strength to tip the balance of debate in Congress at a decisive moment. Years after those historic days, Thomas Jefferson wrote that the Declaration of Independence was intended to serve as "an expression of the American mind." What has not been made clear before now is the critical and indispensable part that the pamphlet *Common Sense* played in turning that American mind toward the thought of independence and in clearing the way to July 4, 1776.

2

" . . . AN ENGLISHMAN"

I t has been said of many of America's founding fathers that they were unlikely revolutionaries, and, compared to men such as Robespierre and Stalin of subsequent epochs, this assertion is largely accurate. Few would have suspected that a cranky, conservative Braintree, Massachusetts, homebody and lawyer was capable or willing to occupy the radical gadfly role he assumed in the Continental Congress—just as no one who knew the shy, bookish scion of Virginia aristocracy would have predicted that he was to become the voice of a nation in rebellion. And yet, time and again, John Adams and Thomas Jefferson proved themselves equal to the extraordinary challenges presented by their nation's crisis. They were revolutionaries not by *nature* or even *nurture* but by the peculiar *necessity* of their times. The same could be said of Washington, Franklin, Madison, and others. But, of all the men who came to play a central role in the founding of America, none was as unlikely as the 37-year-old former corset maker, failed shopkeeper, and cashiered tax collector who arrived in the colonies on November 30, 1774, aboard a typhoid-ridden ship named the *London Packet*.

In fact, if not for another in the series of lucky breaks, the future author of *Common Sense* and *The American Crisis* might not have lived long enough to set foot upon American soil. Hearing that

Paine carried introductions from the world-renowned Philadelphian Benjamin Franklin, a local doctor had the deathly ill man carried ashore and nursed him back to health. Thomas Paine's run of good fortune, brief as it was, carried him from the slums of London to the bustling city of Philadelphia, then known as the *capital of the new world*. The rest would be up to him. His 3,000-mile trip had taken him from a stale, hidebound world where a man's birth dictated the scope of the life that was available to him, to a new land where a man could go as far as ambition, hard work, and genius could take him. The change would profoundly alter the course of Thomas Paine's life. He, in return, would profoundly alter the future of his adopted homeland.

It is worth noting here that efforts to explore the early life and career of Thomas Paine prior to his sailing for North America should remain wary of the work of several so called "biographers" who are better described as hatchet men hired by the British government in the 1790s to discredit the man who had become such a painful thorn in their side. Nevertheless, it is possible to piece together a reasonably complete narrative from the available sources.

Thomas Paine's life began on January 29, 1737, in a small brick house on Bridge Street in the town of Thetford, County Norfolk. About seventy miles north of London, the quiet, pastoral town boasted a long history even by Old World standards. In fact, the birth of Thomas Paine was not the first time the obscure town of Thetford had stood witness to an important moment in the annals of colonial rebellion. Seventeen centuries earlier, according to local tradition, the people of this east Anglican countryside had taken up arms in the Boudiccan uprising, which shook the throne of the most powerful empire of *their* day. In A.D. 60, after a stunning series of bloody victories, an army consisting of several allied indigenous British tribes was finally defeated and annihilated by the legions of Nero's Rome. Time would, of course, accomplish what the barbarian forces could not. Soon after the end of the Roman presence in Britain in the fifth century, the foundations of modern Thetford were laid, and by the eleventh century the town of Thetford was one of the largest in Britain.

By 1737, while not so much in decline, agricultural Thetford had been largely eclipsed by many of the thriving new towns that had grown up around more modern industries such as manufacturing and coal mining. A young boy might have had little reason to rue the fact that his place of birth had become an economic and political backwater. In fact, that obscurity may have been in part a blessing, as Thetford's agriculture-based economy remained largely immune to the price and wage vicissitudes that buffeted Britain's larger, more industrialized towns during the middle of the eighteenth century. There were fields and meadows to occupy a young boy's time and a diversity of wildlife to animate his curiosity. In contrast to the over-crowded, impoverished, smog-choked conditions evident in more modern towns, Paine's birthplace was a close-knit agricultural community whose pace followed the ancient cycle of seasonal renewal from planting to cultivation to harvest and back again. And yet, for all its idyllic charm, the Thetford area was not without evidence of social dissension, division, and inequity. The surrounding country-side was littered with ruins of monasteries, priories, and chapels marking different phases of England's religious struggles. Politically, it was a typical example of the arbitrary nature of the English form of constitutional government. Of the town's roughly two thousand inhabitants, just thirty-one men were eligible to vote—and those only for the parliamentary candidates endorsed by the Duke of Grafton. Paine would later ridicule the inequality of the British con-stitutional monarchy:

> The county of Yorkshire, which contains near a million
> souls, sends two county members [to Parliament]; and so

does the county of Rutland, which contains not an hundredth part of that number. The town of old Sarum, which contains not three houses, sends two members; and the town of Manchester, which contains upwards of sixty thousand souls, is not permitted to send any.

(Indeed the town of Dunwich still returned two members in spite of the fact that it had long been submerged under the North Sea.) Paine knew well that inequities such as these did not arise naturally. They were created intentionally by influential aristocrats who wanted to further manipulate a system that was already stacked in their favor. Upon arriving in the colonies, Paine often found himself at odds with American loyalists who, from a distance of three thousand miles, had formed a more favorable notion of the merits of the British constitutional monarchy than his own.

Thomas Paine's father was a devout Quaker and an established Thetford tradesman named Joseph Pain. (Thomas adopted the *e* in America at the beginning of his career as a political writer.) Joseph must have been a man of singular decency and rectitude, for even Thomas Paine's most bilious "biographers" have not been able to conjure up anything ill to say of him. Paine's mother was Frances Cocke, eleven years older than Joseph, the daughter of an attorney and, as such, a member of Thetford's upper class. Also in contrast to her husband, Frances was a devout follower of the established Church of England. Since Joseph's chosen profession, corset-making, was not one of the more prestigious of the skilled trades and only just kept his family in middle-class fashion, Frances certainly married below her station—whether out of love or out of some less sentimental necessity is unknown.

The chief work of a corset-maker was the crafting of the steel or whalebone stays that provided rigid support for the undergarments preferred by fashionable women of the day. It was physically demanding work, requiring considerable strength as well as manual dexterity. In later years, acquaintances of the famous writer would remark upon his facility with tools and the nimbleness of his hands—traits no doubt honed in his father's shop.

Joseph and Frances, however, had greater hopes for their only son than for him to follow the usual path into his father's trade. At the age of six, unlike most boys of his age and station, young Thomas was enrolled in the local grammar school. His parents shouldered this considerable sacrifice because they knew that education was the one key by which the son of a humble tradesman could gain access into the more exalted professions of law, medicine, and the clergy. Unfortunately for the young scholar, a key component of the required curriculum was a mastery of Latin, a subject in which he would show little aptitude.

While his grammar school career lasted only six years, it was nonetheless an important formative experience in Paine's life, one whose influence he would later cite frequently. Among the specific incidents he would recall, several would have a direct impact on the course of his life for good and ill. One irresponsible instructor repeatedly rhapsodized on the subject of his own youthful adventures aboard a Man-of-War, which inspired at least one of his impressionable charges to follow a similar dangerous path. A separate experience planted the desire for another journey that Paine would make almost twenty-five years later:

> I happened, when a school boy, to pick up a pleasing natural history of Virginia, and my inclination from that day of seeing the western side of the Atlantic never left me.

It was also during his grammar school years that the young Paine evinced some of the innate interests and talents that would have such a pivotal effect on his later life. Ironically, Paine seems to have felt a mixture of indifference and embarrassment when he dis-covered that he possessed a natural aptitude for writing, especially poetry. Instead, as Paine would relate, "The natural bent of my mind was to science." His passion for science would remain with him throughout his life, leading him into explorations as varied as the development of smokeless candles, the causes of yellow fever, and the principles of iron bridge architecture. It would also influence his unsentimental view of and approach to the social, political, and gov-ernance issues he would tackle in his most famous works.

But, for all his application to the subjects that interested him, the requisite mastery of Latin remained stubbornly elusive. Without it, his parents' hopes for a future doctor, lawyer, or clergyman were in vain. The idea of knowledge for knowledge's sake not being in vogue at the time, this deficit resulted in the early termination of his education. Later, Paine would ascribe his Latin deficiency both to a streak of Quakerism, which recoiled at anything that smacked of "popery," as well as his general impatience with the "barren study of a dead language." Whatever the cause, at the age of thirteen Thomas Paine found himself bound in his father's shop as an appren-tice stay-maker.

Thomas Paine's parents may have regarded his educational adventure as a vexing and expensive failure, but his brief education may well have laid the foundation for the unexpected accomplish-ments for which he would become famous. His formal education had indeed been derailed prematurely by his lack of facility in Latin, but he had learned to read and write. More importantly, he had been introduced to the world of science and, thereby, to the relatively new belief that all human questions could be approached by human reason. But what would become of this inclination without the encourage-ment of further schooling? His incomplete education meant that he had acquired the fundamental tools of inquiry without assimilating the general system of received knowledge that characterized most educated young men of the day. When it came time for him to apply himself to the larger questions of his time, Thomas Paine came to them unburdened by contemporary assumptions, possessing instead both an ability and inclination to answer them for himself.

Paine does not seem to have particularly minded the change in his circumstances from scholar to apprentice stay-maker. In fact, his later recollections of working with his father are uniformly fond ones. He credited his Quaker father with instilling in him "a tolerable stock of useful learning" as well as "an exceedingly good moral education." The useful learning included the skills of a trade that would support him on and off over the next twenty years. His "moral education" would have an even more profound and permanent influence on the man he would become.

The central tenet of Quaker belief is reliance upon a personal "inner light" spirituality as opposed to the dictates of scriptural dogma and ecclesiastical authorities. Often described as a "divine spark" bestowed by God upon every human being, this spiritual light, Quakers hold, is a constant presence, influencing people to resist evil and to do good works. While he never became a practicing Quaker, Paine often expressed a similar belief in the essential goodness of mankind, as well as a lifelong commitment to public service. Throughout most of his adult years, however, the man who would become famous (and infamous) for his deistic beliefs, frequently identified himself as a Quaker. Many of the values and moral positions he would adopt in life and defend in his writings can be seen as echoes of his early Quaker influence.

Refusing to accept the Anglican Church's Thirty-Nine Articles of Faith, Quakers were seen, and saw themselves, as dissenters or outsiders. Throughout his life, Paine, too, seemed comfortable in the role of a non-conformist—whether in religion, politics, or any other matter—when the established dogma ran counter to empirical evidence. While they were no longer targets of open persecution as in the seventeenth century, Quakers were still banned from voting, holding public office, or attending the state universities at Oxford and Cambridge. Paine's lifelong mistrust of governmental and ecclesiastic power can easily be seen as a response to this discrimination, as can his early advocacy of abolition, religious tolerance, and universal suffrage.

Another result of his father's religious influence was a thorough knowledge of biblical texts. Paine maintained an ability to quote long passages of scripture from memory, and this proficiency would later serve him well in making the case for American independence to a population reared in the puritan tradition for which scripture was an unanswerable authority.

Aside from his affectionate relationship with his father, the years spent in a corset shop must have, on some level, been unrewarding ones—particularly if the teenage Paine possessed any of the qualities, such as ambition and a desire for recognition, that would mark the adult. More importantly, the long-term outcome of his apprenticeship was far from certain. While Thetford could sustain one master corset-maker in modest style, there was clearly not enough work to support two. With his father still a relatively young man at 41, Paine's future seemed to lie beyond the familiar boundaries of his hometown.

Still, his desire to strike out on his own blossomed more quickly than his father might have wished. The year was 1756, and the Seven Years War against the French was just beginning. At "little more than 16 years of age," recalled Paine, the young man ran away to join the crew of a privateer, heeding visions instilled by his erstwhile schoolmaster. Privateers, during the frequent European conflicts of that era, operated as freelance pirate ships to which the individual European powers gave permission to harass their enemies at sea, extending their naval forces without additional cost. These legalized corsairs operated with the blessing of the country they represented as expressed in a commission called a *Letter of Marque*. While, like a pirate ship, a privateer's crew received a share of captured booty—cargo and money—the greatest value of any capture was usually the vessel itself. To realize that profit, however, the ship had to be sailed back to a friendly port and sold at auction. For this reason, ships captured by a privateer, together with their crews and passengers, were usually treated with more leniency than at the hands of ordinary pirates. At other times, unfortunately, it was a distinction without a difference. A privateer's crew often counted unreconstructed pirates among their company, and more than one opportunistic ship pursued its business alternating their status from pirate to privateer as the shifting European political situation allowed.

To learn the story of Paine's running away to sea is almost to be convinced that Fate, itself, had set out to teach the young man a lesson by means of a vast morality play. The ship young Thomas Paine had agreed to set sail upon was ominously named the *Terrible*, under the command of the almost implausibly named William Death. The fate of Captain Death and his unfortunate ship should come as no surprise to anyone. Soon after setting sail from England, the *Terrible* engaged the French privateer *Vengeance*. In a fierce battle both ships were heavily damaged, and the *Terrible* lost over one hundred and fifty crewmen, including almost all of her officers and, of course, her commander, Captain Death. Only seventeen of the *Terrible*'s crewmen survived. Luckily for Paine, and for history, the eighteen-year-old runaway was not aboard. His father had hurried to London after him and, finding him signed on to the privateer, applied "the affectionate and good moral remonstrance of a good father," as Paine would later write, ultimately convincing his son to abandon his plan and return home. In relating this story, Paine seemed to have felt a measure of remorse, confessing that his kind, upright Quaker father "must begin to look upon me as lost."

Even so, the lure of the sea was not easily put off, especially for an imaginative, ambitious young man whose prospects in life were otherwise quite limited. Before the year was out, even after reading newspaper accounts of the *Terrible*'s misfortune, the young man was ready to try again. In his second attempt, however, Paine was more successful—both in his choice of a ship and in following through with his plans. The *King of Prussia*, under the command of a Captain Mendez, was a large ship for a privateer, with two gun decks and a crew of 250. While it is not known how many engagements the ship fought while Paine was aboard, she recorded nine captured ships with their cargoes. In addition to a modest salary, every crewman received a share of the proceeds from captured prizes. Even as an ordinary seaman, Paine's share for his time on the ship worked out to more than thirty pounds a year—about what his father made as a master stay-maker. In spite of this windfall of good luck and although the war would last another five years, Paine decided not to re-enlist.

While Paine never wrote of the details of his nearly two years aboard the *King of Prussia*, there is no doubt that he saw a good share of death and destruction. Many years later he would denounce the practice of privateering in general for its lawless disruption of international commerce as "The channels of trade broken up, the high road of the seas infested with robbers of every nation." Nonetheless, it was an important experience for the young man. He traveled, faced enemy fire, and learned to keep his head in times of extreme danger. Although he would later count among his friends esteemed military leaders like Washington, General Nathanial Greene, and the Marquis de Lafayette, it was this time, his own "two years before the mast" aboard the *King of Prussia*, that honed Paine's unequaled insight to the hearts and minds of rank-and-file soldiers—their fears, their hopes, and what they fought for. On more than one occasion during the Revolution, with his troops facing low morale, bad weather, hunger, and impossible odds, General Washington would steel his soldiers' hearts by reading to them the words of Thomas Paine.

After brief stints as a journeyman stay-maker, first in London and then Dover, Paine was able to put together the funds he needed to set up his own business. He set up shop in the coastal town of Sandwich as a master stay-maker and soon thereafter, in September of 1759, married the pretty Mary Lambert. While he seems to have been a talented, hardworking craftsman, Paine's business instincts left much to be desired. In what would become only the first of a series of testaments to this fact, the young couple was soon forced to flee a mounting pile of debts, settling eventually in Margate, a little farther up the coast. Tragedy pursued them, however, and within a year Mary died—whether from long illness or complications during childbirth is not known. This succession of misfortune seems to have set young Paine back on his heels. He abandoned the trade that was his only means of support and cast about for a new vocation.

His late wife's father had been an officer in the excise service and persuaded Paine to pursue the same career. The salary of an "exciseman" was not a generous one, but it was a steady position and admission was competitive—requiring a degree of patronage as well as a rigorous written examination. Paine returned to his father's home to prepare for the test, which he passed, and was admitted to the service on December 1, 1762. Although he was officially an excise officer, he had to wait for a position to become available before he could assume a post—and get paid. He waited until August of 1764, when he was appointed to the town of Alford in Lincolnshire. His beat was a large district—surrounding the town and hugging the northeast coast of England—known as the Alford *Out-Ride*, a territory covered by an officer on horseback.

The excise tax was an onerous duty that fell with disproportionate weight upon the poorer classes of Englishmen. It was levied upon goods such as tobacco and alcohol, as well as essentials like salt and soap. Despised by the people who had to pay the tax and threat-ened by the smugglers who tried to evade it, an excise officer's job was often a dangerous one, especially on a sprawling, isolated post like the Alford Out-Ride. Nor was it lucrative, considering the expense of maintaining a permanent residence in addition to the stable and lodging fees entailed by their almost continual travel.

It was a frequent complaint of excise officers that such demands on their resources, combined with the unceasing nature of their work, often led to diminished performance—meaning inattention at best and outright fraud at worst. A common instance of the former was the practice of "stamping the whole ride" or assessing a tax based on an incomplete survey of the goods. Common as it may have been, it was still punished harshly when detected, even upon a first offense. Paine would learn this the hard way only a year after assuming his post. As the official complaint against him read, Paine was found guilty of assessing a certain "victualler's stocks" without inspecting the individual items and, consequently, "ordered to be discharged."

There was no suggestion of dishonesty, however, only hastiness, and, under such circumstances, dismissal was not necessarily per-manent. In the interval before he could apply for re-admittance to the service, Paine returned briefly, and no doubt reluctantly, to stay-making before finding a position teaching English at a London academy run by Daniel Noble, a local elder and preacher. Unfortunately, Paine recorded little about his experiences as a teacher—whether he enjoyed it or how his relationship was with his students. (One of his former pupils, on a tour of America, visited Paine in Philadelphia during the war. Paine was glad to see the young man and wrote him an introduction to Washington.) The salary of a teacher, however, was even less than that of a customs officer, and so, after a second brief tenure at a school in Kensington, Paine wrote what he called a humble petition to the excise board. His appeal was granted, and he was reinstated in July of 1767. Declining the first position offered him, Paine eventually accepted an appointment to the town of Lewes, County Sussex in February 1768.

Paine's second spell as a custom's officer, like his second attempt to go to sea, proved a far more rewarding one than the first. He would remain in Lewes for six years, marry the daughter of one of the town's leading families, earn the esteem of his peers and superiors within the excise service, and find support within a stimulating community of like-minded companions. It was in Lewes that he began to gain the confidence he would need to develop and publicize his thoughts on the political and social issues of the day.

His second wife, Elizabeth, was the daughter of a Samuel Ollive, owner of a local general store, former town constable, and onetime proprietor of the White Hart Tavern—the social and political nexus of the town. Paine rented rooms from the Ollives, and when Samuel died 1769, Paine offered to help Mrs. Ollive and her daughter, Elizabeth, keep the store running. While Paine's commercial "skills" did little to help the business thrive, something else did manage to flourish. In what seems to have been an act of convenience for both parties, Thomas and Elizabeth were married on March 26, 1771.

While the excise tax was no more popular in Lewes than it was anywhere else in England, Paine used his humorous, sympathetic manner to deflect his neighbors' animosity and became quite popular throughout the town, winning "many friends, rich and poor." It must have been a difficult balance to maintain during a time of growing social unrest and economic hardship throughout the countryside. In fact, as he later wrote, his position as a tax collector afforded him a firsthand view of "the numerous and various distresses which the weight of taxes even at that time of day occasioned." A series of bad harvests led to an uncertain food supply and rising prices. Instead of alleviating the problems, the government of George III, facing its own financial crisis due in part to the extraordinary expense of the French and Indian War in North America, levied even more burdensome taxes on the British people. Far from immune, the excise officers themselves were particularly vulnerable to the shifting economic climate. One of the arguments Thomas Paine would later make on their behalf was that, as the cost of their expenses rose, officers could not pass on the increase by raising their fees accordingly. Their salaries were fixed by the government and could only be raised by government action. Whatever the merits of their case, trying to provoke that action would turn out to be a frustrating and embittering experience—both for the officers and for their chief spokesman.

Personally, however, Paine was enjoying perhaps the happiest years of his life up to then. This was due mostly to the social connections he formed within the Lewes community, particularly those that centered on the White Hart Tavern. Occupying a central place in the life of the town, it not only was an informal meeting place but also functioned as the seat of the town council that oversaw local elections and appointments. Taking what would be his first active role in practical politics, Paine served on the council and became an established figure in the regular discussions and debates of the tavern's Headstrong Club. His fellow members were, as a contemporary reported, "a very respectable, sensible, and convivial set of acquaintances." Paine seems to have entered into this small community of friends with great enthusiasm, participating in debates with such frequency and ardor that he was remembered as the most regular recipient of the club's Headstrong Book—an "old Greek Homer" that was awarded to the winner of each evening's rhetorical combat. Indeed, the "commodore," as he was known in recognition of his brief career at sea, became a popular figure among these men, "who were entertained by his witty sallies, and informed by his more serious conversations."

What the specific subjects of these more serious conversations consisted of can only be guessed, but Paine soon grew confident enough in his voice and in what he had to say that he began to seek a wider audience. Among the pieces that he wrote at this time, two enjoyed considerable local success. The first was a poem written on or about the tenth anniversary of the death of General James Wolfe outside Quebec during the French and Indian War. While the subject of the epic poem was Wolfe's heroic death and ascension into heaven, its tone and language were ironically supportive of the mythology and glory of the British Empire, which Paine would so effectively assail only a few years later in America.

His other well-received effort from this period was less serious in style but more political in its ultimate message. "Farmer Short's Dog Porter" told the humorous tale of a humble farmer who ran afoul of three local justices of the peace. His crime? The poor farmer had unwisely cast his vote for a candidate other than the ones supported by the three vindictive justices. As a result the farmer and his dog are persecuted, hauled before the bench on trumped up charges, and sentenced to hang. Although much fun is made of the justices' drunkenness and the *sang froid* with which they condemn both man and beast, it is easy to perceive a seething resentment of corrupt government, perverted justice, and arbitrary power running just beneath the surface levity.

Paine's efforts won him a reputation as a writer of some talent, as well as a more concrete emolument. A candidate for a neighboring parliamentary seat approached Paine and offered him three guineas to write a campaign song for the upcoming election. While it is uncertain whether this was an isolated commission, it was the first instance of Paine, then in his mid-thirties, employing his literary gift as an instrument of political persuasion. It may be more, or less, than coincidence that the candidate, a man named Rumbold, was a Whig and that it was radical members of the Whig party who were the most ardent champions of the American cause within the British government.

As well as things may have been going for Thomas Paine, socially and professionally, these were far from halcyon times around

Lewes and throughout England. Sussex was representative of other counties during this period of economic hardship and unrest, which history described as "a record of poverty, disaster and lawlessness." Falling wages and food shortages combined with mounting taxation stretched the sufferance of the English people to the breaking point. Outbreaks of public discord became more frequent, and radical politicians gained in popularity as they waxed more audacious in their criticism of the government. Opposition figures such as the infamous John Wilkes used the new medium of the popular press to appeal directly to the British people—publicizing controversial opinions and attacking political enemies with increasing impunity.

Far from immune to these economic gyrations, the condition of the excise officers was particularly tenuous. In contrast to unhappy silk-weavers and coal heavers who went on strike in protest during this period, the excise men decided to register their discontent through more conventional channels. In 1772, the 3,000 or so officers decided to press their case before Parliament and contributed three shillings each to create a war chest of 500 pounds. In a testament to his standing within the service, as well as his reputation as a gifted writer and resolute polemicist, the 35-year-old Paine was asked to craft the officials' petition to Parliament. He initially refused, then reconsidered and accepted the assignment. In a general way, Paine's "Case of the Officers of Excise" presaged *Common Sense* more than any of his earlier works had; it, too, was written on behalf of a disgruntled constituency, addressed to a specific audience, and intended to provoke a particular response. By all accounts, Paine's first pamphlet received widespread approbation throughout the excise department and even amongst outside readers. A 4,000-copy print run was ordered, and Paine himself was sent to London to push the case before Parliament.

The pamphlet's line of argument stayed fairly close to the central issue: that the officers' salary, once deductions were made for their expenses, was no longer adequate for their needs. Paine wrote that the "increase of money in the kingdom"—inflation—placed an unfair burden upon civil servants who did not have the freedom to adjust their salaries accordingly. He also warned that the officers' increasing hardship led to a decrease in the quality of their work and consequently in the amount of tax revenue the government would receive. Paine found creative ways to emphasize these basic premises again and again, each time looking at them from a slightly different perspective. He appealed alternately to his audience's pragmatism, their sense of fair play, and their enlightened self-interest. For obvious reasons, the tone of the pamphlet was far more deferential than that of *Common Sense*. Only once, when he lamented that the "ease and affluence" of a privileged few should be built upon the "misfortune of others," did he pick up a quasi-adversarial tone and seem to forecast one of the major themes of his later work. While in this earlier piece the aggrieved were common Englishmen rather than American colonists, the British ruling elite played the same part they would later in *Common Sense*. The main difference between the two pamphlets arose from the fact that this earlier work was directed at the system rather than against it. Here he was trying to persuade the British government. Later he would be trying to revile it.

Paine left for London in the winter of 1772, no doubt confident of his work on the petition and consequently of achieving his comrades' just aims of a pay raise. But, as Paine would soon learn, the will of the British government during this period was not swayed by sound logic or just arguments. A jaded political veteran such as Benjamin Franklin, then in London representing the colonies of Massachusetts and Pennsylvania, could have saved him the disappointment. Unlike the naïve Englishman, the famous American knew that success in such cases depended too often on the support of powerful friends and interested parties within the government. In representing a group of investors attempting to acquire a large tract of land in the Ohio Valley, Franklin recommended that they offer shares in the project to persons of influence at court and in Parliament. Without such maneuvers, Franklin told his partners, their cause didn't stand a chance. Such facts must have come as harsh realizations to Paine, still innocent in the ways of government. In spite of the fact that his pamphlet was well written, generally praised, and widely circulated, the campaign for a salary increase came to naught. As he later summarized bitterly, " . . . the King, or somebody for him, applied to Parliament to have his own salary raised 100,000 pounds, which being done, everything else was laid aside."

In spite of the failure of its original objective, the year or so Paine spent in London was not without some reward. He had succeeded in making a good impression on the commissioner of the excise board, a man named George Lewis Scott. Scott was not only an influential man in the excise department, but also a celebrated amateur mathematician and scientist. Many years earlier he had been a tutor of George III, and Paine later credited Scott for apprising him of "the true character of the present King." Perhaps more significantly, Scott also provided his new friend with *entrée* into a distinguished circle of acquaintances that included writers Samuel Johnson and Edward Gibbon, as well as numerous men who, like Paine and Scott, shared an at-least amateur interest in science and philosophical inquiry. But the most illustrious member of Scott's circle would also prove to be the most significant friendship Paine would ever have. In addition to his duties as a colonial agent and other business pursuits, Benjamin Franklin was an active member of Scott's circle, as well as his good friend.

Thomas Paine, actively pushing the excise officers' claim in London throughout the winter of 1772–73, also found time to attend scientific lectures and immerse himself in the city's rich intellectual atmosphere. The active principle animating the London science community during this period was the Newtonian belief that no assumption was too fundamental, and no subject too sacred, to be beyond the reach of reason and scientific inquiry. For them every observable phenomenon was susceptible to Newton's process of hypothesis and experimentation, from gravity and planetary movement to the nature of God. Nor were received notions about politics and government immune to their searching skepticism. Not surprisingly their willingness to question the policies and institutions of their government made them a natural breeding ground for radical and opposition politics. In fact, one of the causes that they would champion long before it took a central place on the international stage was regarding the rights of British Americans. Drawn into their company by his scientific and mathematical interests, Thomas Paine also imbibed a healthy dose of the political theories he would take with him to America.

One of the more famous of these intellectual cabals was the "Club of Honest Whigs" with which Franklin was associated. In addition to their scientific, political, and religious interests, the Honest Whigs were early supporters of the cause of the American colonies. While it is not known for certain how much, or even if, Paine had contact with the Honest Whigs, he was certainly influenced by their thinking. Two of them in particular, a schoolmaster named James Burgh and the influential clergyman and political commentator Joseph Priestley, had a direct impact on Paine's thought and are referenced in the pages of *Common Sense*.

One thing that is known about Paine's movements in London is that he met and became friends with Dr. Franklin. Even apart from their mutual interests in science and mathematics, it is easy to see what may have inspired the world-renowned inventor and philosopher to take an interest in Paine. While the humble excise officer and budding writer had nothing in the way of Franklin's extraordinary accomplishments, the same could be said of all but a few men. But, like Paine, Franklin's origins were inauspicious. Both men were self-educated. Both men were brought up in middle-class homes, the sons of humble tradesmen. Both men balked at the prospect of serving an apprenticeship in their father's shop. Both men attempted to ship out on a privateer only to be talked out of it on the wharf by their concerned fathers. And ultimately both did find their fortunes far from the place of their birth. Even considering all these parallels in their pasts, neither of them could have guessed at the time the extent to which their future paths would become intertwined. Unlike Franklin, who was admired by kings and counted among his friends the most prominent intellects of the eighteenth century, Paine would be profoundly affected by this friendship. He idolized Franklin and no doubt drew inspiration from the achievements of this great man whose beginnings were so similar to his own.

It is fortunate that Paine spent his spare time in London to such worthwhile effect; for, his involvement in the excise officers' case would cost him dearly. While Paine's lack of business acumen had not done much for the fortunes of the small shop he helped his wife and mother-in-law run, his absence from the shop proved even more damaging. Not long after his return to Lewes, the Ollives' grocery business foundered, and the shop together with its contents were sold at auction. Paine's odd marriage, which had always seemed an extension of a business relationship, ended a month later, without rancor or, it seems, any other emotion. Thomas and Elizabeth never officially divorced, and neither ever remarried. Years later, his finances much improved, Paine would send anonymous assistance to her when she was in need.

In spite of receiving praise from his superiors for his handling of the excise officers' case and for his work in general, Paine was again dismissed from the service in April of 1774. Dismissal came as a hard blow to the 37-year-old Paine, who, already disappointed over the loss of the case, saw it as an arbitrary and petty act of retribution against a loyal servant. In all likelihood, it was his bitter memory of this episode, in part, that led him to publish *Common Sense* anonymously. It is not difficult to trace his anger and bitterness toward the British government—sentiments that pervaded much of his later writing—to this sad denouement of what had been an otherwise bright period in Paine's life. Within a few years' time, an English commentator would have occasion to lament that the dismissal of this one customs officer may have cost Great Britain her colonies.

With nothing holding him in Lewes, Paine returned to London. Once there, he seems to have decided almost immediately (with Benjamin Franklin's strong encouragement) upon a plan to travel to the American colonies. With his share of the proceeds from the general store's auction, Paine was able to purchase first-class passage to Philadelphia aboard the *London Packet*. Franklin wrote two last-minute letters of introduction: one to his son-in-law, Philadelphia merchant Richard Bache (pronounced "beech"), and the second to his own son William, the royal governor of New Jersey. He vouched for "Thomas Pain" as an "ingenious worthy young man" whom they should endeavor to help obtain employment and thereby "much oblige your affectionate father." The *London Packet*, carrying Paine, rode down the Thames in October 1774, rounded Land's End, and pointed a course for North America. As the land of his birth sank below the horizon, Paine's memories of failure, disappointment, and bitterness receded before what must have been a new sense of hope for his future in a new country. Paine would not return to England until 1787, when would be a different man and the world a different place. At the age of 37, Thomas Paine, a poor and obscure Englishman by any account, departed the old world for the new. By the time he returned in 1787, Edmund Burke could refer to him accurately as the "great American." In the intervening 14 years, Paine would find a calling, England would lose a war, and the meaning of the term "American" would be changed forever.

3

THE CAPITAL OF THE NEW WORLD

After an uneventful passage across the north Atlantic and the 100-mile trip up the Delaware River, the *London Packet* placed its anchor in the mud of the New World on November 30, 1774. Founded by William Penn as a Quaker colony in 1682, the city of Philadelphia had expanded to occupy the entire stretch of land between the western shore of the Delaware and the eastern banks of the much smaller Schuylkill River. In spite of its relative youth, a population of more than 30,000 ranked it above older colonial rivals and second only to London in the entire British Empire. It was from the start a thoroughly intentional city—laid out in a neat grid in marked contrast to the haphazard character of most cities at the time. John Adams, writing just a few months before Paine's arrival, recorded his first impression in his diary:

> The Regularity and Elegance of this City are very striking. It is situated upon a Neck of Land, about two Miles wide between the River Delaware and the River Schuilkill. The Streets are all exactly straight and parrallell to the River. Front Street is near the River, then 2d

street, 3d, 4th, 5th, 6th, 7th, 8th, 9th. The cross Streets
which intersect these are all equally wide, straight and
parallell to each other, and are named from forrest and
fruit Trees, Pear Street, Apple Street, Walnut Street,
Chestnut Street, &c.

At a time when the leading cities of Europe were marred by san-
itary conditions that had improved little since medieval times,
Philadelphia boasted residential garbage removal and a regular street
cleaning service. It was by far the most cosmopolitan city in the
colonies, with a steady stream of European visitors and immigrants,
as well as trade vessels from around the globe and a religiously
diverse population. A rich cultural schedule of plays, music, art
exhibits, and scientific lectures was patronized by a very wealthy
class of merchants and a growing, prosperous middle class.

Politically, Philadelphia was something of a paradox at that
time. A relatively large population of middle-class artisans who were
just awakening into political consciousness provided a fertile breeding ground for progressive and radical politics. As in London, this
political radicalism was often intertwined with an active scientific
community. At the same time, however, the city was perhaps the
largest bastion of loyalist sentiment in America. The city's wealthy,
influential population of importers and exporters was generally
opposed to any disruption to what was for them a lucrative status quo.
In addition, the city's large Quaker community was conscientiously
opposed to violence and anything that might provoke it. It was the
Quakers who began the practice of referring to the pro-independence
party in Congress as "the Violent People." Whatever their personal
politics, Quakers as a group stood in staunch opposition to any
action or idea that increased the chance of war with England.

Another unique feature of Philadelphia that contributed to its
loyalist sentiments was the presence on the political scene of the

Proprietary party. These descendants of William Penn and their supporters still wielded considerable power over the affairs of Philadelphia by virtue of the original royal charter. Consequently, where other colonists complained of the stifling power of the British, Pennsylvanians found a more immediate annoyance in the Proprietors. In fact, the most common tactic in their efforts to challenge and erode the Proprietors' authority was to support and increase the direct influence of the crown in their political affairs. When the climate began to change and the rift between the colonies and Great Britain widened, many Pennsylvanians found themselves torn between their traditional loyalty to the crown and a growing sense of duty to their country.

In 1774, this most sophisticated of American cities was itself poised on a precipice between modernity and the vestiges of English feudalism. The top ten percent of Philadelphia's wealthiest citizens owned more than half the city's wealth and exerted an even more disproportionate influence over local government. These people tended to have more in common with their British counterparts across the Atlantic than with the ordinary citizens across town. They followed British fashions, read British magazines and newspapers, and tended to view colonial affairs through British rather than American eyes.

An even more stark inequity was evidenced in the large number of unpaid laborers—slaves, apprentices, and indentured servants. Estimates place the number as equal to that of paid, free laborers. By the time Paine arrived in Philadelphia, however, these conditions were already in flux. As the emerging class of artisans grew in numbers and wealth, they began to seek a commensurate enlargement of their political rights and influence. The decline of the slave trade and an increasing number of those reaching the end of their indenture swelled the ranks of independent wage-earners who would gradually seek their own political and economic interests. These trends toward a more egalitarian society would no doubt have played out in one way or another over the next several decades—just as they would in many European cities. But the coming of the Revolution would accelerate the transformation to such an extent that, by the end of the war, Philadelphians could justly say that they lived in a thoroughly modern city.

On September 5, 1774, Philadelphia took center stage in the progress of colonial events when the first Continental Congress convened in the city's Carpenter Hall. Fifty-six delegates from twelve of the colonies (except Georgia) met to formulate a coordinated colonial response to the latest attempts by the British Parliament to enforce their control over colonial affairs. At the top of the colonists' list of grievances were the Intolerable Acts, a series of punitive measures passed by Parliament in the spring of '74 and designed to repay colonial defiance of previous acts. Showing undiminished defiance, the congressional delegates went about their work quickly. In a flurry of legislative activity, the Congress declared thirteen parliamentary acts unconstitutional and agreed to impose economic sanctions against the British until they were repealed. They also drew up a declaration of colonial rights and committed to reconvene in May of 1775 to assess the progress of their dispute. The tensions and debates at play within Carpenter Hall had inevitably spilled out into the surrounding streets, providing plentiful grist for the mill of Philadelphia's vibrant, unfettered press.

Just one month after the Congress had dissolved, the stricken *London Packet* sat anchored in the city's harbor. Of the 125 who had booked passage, 80 had fallen ill with what appears to have been typhus. A physician named John Kearsley came aboard to observe the desperate condition of the passengers and crew. As he made his rounds, there was little he could do for the sufferers—they would have to stay aboard the ship until either they died or their illness passed. But a well-dressed man, occupying one of the ship's five first-class cabin berths, attracted special attention when it was discovered that he carried letters from Dr. Franklin in London. Out of respect for the esteemed scientist, philosopher and Philadelphian, Dr. Kearsley ordered that the unconscious man be placed in his launch and rowed ashore.

Thomas Paine lay in bed for six weeks before he was pronounced fully restored. The convalescent had not been completely idle though. He had made several acquaintances, read the local newspapers, and already absorbed a thorough sense of the political winds at large in the city. Remarkably, Paine's first political essay was written while he was still in his sickbed. In the "Dialogue Between General Wolfe and General Gage in a Wood near Boston," Paine demonstrated a shrewd grasp of the central grievances driving the colonists' dissatisfaction. As one modern commentator notes, "The piece was almost *too* American." Demonstrating Paine's uncanny ability to gauge and address the mood of his audience, the essay also strongly suggests that Paine's thinking on the growing conflict between Great Britain and the colonies had begun before he crossed the Atlantic. Quite strikingly, Paine's first political essay reveals something else about its author. At the time Paine wrote, Americans still valued their relationship to the king, even while they fulminated against the Parliament. But Paine denied the separation between the two, suggesting that at least some of the colonists "have not only thrown off the jurisdiction of the British Parliament, but they are disaffected to the British crown."

It was mid-January before Paine called on Richard Bache, a successful businessman married to Benjamin and Deborah Franklin's only daughter, Sarah. He was well connected in Philadelphia society due both to his famous father-in-law and his own outgoing nature. Bache made inquiries on Paine's behalf and seems to have had little trouble finding tutoring work for the recently arrived Englishman. He also introduced him to Robert Aitken, a printer and the proprietor of a small bookshop. Aitken, a recent Scots immigrant, was known in the city for the quality of his work. He would later publish the *Journals of the Continental Congress* and be commissioned by Congress to produce "The First American Bible" when the war cut off access to imported editions. At the time he met Paine, the printer-publisher was in the midst of launching a new monthly called *Pennsylvania Magazine*, styled after the popular English magazines.

The magazine as a medium was barely half a century old, the first being the work of an entrepreneurial London printer named Edward Cave, who named this premier monthly the *Gentlemen's Magazine*. As the latter word implies, Cave intended his new publication to be a collection or *warehouse* containing a diverse inventory of news, ideas, and useful information then in circulation throughout England. The *Gentleman's Magazine*, like its future American emulators, featured some original pieces along with many reprints, excerpts, or adaptations of other publications.

Due to a scarcity of homegrown sources, previous American magazines had contained mostly English reprints. Aitken wanted his *Pennsylvania Magazine* to be a truly American publication, featuring original work from American writers. Paine welcomed the opportunity to join the new venture, and the two men struck a partnership deal. They agreed that the magazine would cover a wide range of subjects, from science to literature to current affairs, while steering clear of controversial areas such as religious and political debates. The arrangement worked to the benefit of both men: Paine gained a steady salary of fifty pounds a year, and Aitken gained an eager, versatile writer at a relatively cheap price.

The first issue, to which Paine made only a few submissions, was greeted by an appreciative, if small, readership. After that Paine became *Pennsylvania Magazine*'s primary contributor, writing under multiple pseudonyms in each issue on topics ranging from science to history to a parable on Alexander the Great.

Under Paine's editorship, the magazine's subscriber list grew from 600 to over 1,500 in just two months, making it the most widely read magazine in the colonies. Benjamin Rush attributed the sharp increase in part to a particularly well-received issue containing Paine's poem on the death of Wolfe, as well as to a highly critical piece about Lord Clive, the man who subdued India for the British Crown. That these two pieces attracted widespread acclaim highlights the fundamental paradox of colonial feeling just before the Revolution. The poem was uncritical imperial propaganda, while the Lord Clive essay was a stinging condemnation of England's mistreatment of a distant colony. That both were simultaneously well-received evinces American colonialism's fragile equilibrium and demonstrates the truth of Paine's recollection that, upon arriving in Philadelphia, "I found the disposition of the people such that might have been lead by a thread and governed by a reed."

During the period of his editorial guidance—from February to June of 1775—Paine's output reflected his pleasure at having found an outlet for his emerging voice. Under various pennames, he wrote, on average, twenty percent of the articles and essays in each issue and edited the rest. While a dull subject usually elicited a dull article, Paine was at his best writing on controversial issues about which he had strong feelings. He wrote passionately in favor of women's rights and the abolition of slavery long before such positions became popular. But he saved his sharpest quills for the subject increasingly close to his heart—the fundamental corruption, venality, and tyranny of the English system of government.

In light of the modest writing experience Paine had gained while in England, the time Paine spent editing and, more importantly, writing for *Pennsylvania Magazine* deserves attention as a critical step in his development into the author of *Common Sense*. Furthermore, the audience Paine would later reach and move so effectively with his pamphlets was to a great extent the same audience he addressed within the pages of *Pennsylvania Magazine*. The success of the magazine—due in part to Paine's writing and in part to a growing appetite for such work especially among Philadelphia's large, literate artisan class—would in many ways prefigure the extraordinary success of *Common Sense*.

The eclectic mix of subjects contained in a typical issue of *Pennsylvania Magazine* mirrored not only the interests of its editor but also of that particular readership. The six issues, from February to July, upon which Paine had the most direct influence, featured articles on plants, animals, medicine, and astronomy, as well as reports about the latest discoveries and inventions. In addition to these interests, Paine was already becoming increasingly, if subtly, preoccupied with the issue upon which he would eventually become the world's most famous commentator: the deteriorating relationship between the colonies and Great Britain.

As Aitken intended, *Pennsylvania Magazine* at first avoided taking partisan positions on divisive political questions. Until the bloodshed at Lexington and Concord on April 19, 1775, his editor paid at least nominal obeisance to this mandate. To be sure, Paine's writing did become more openly anti-British after what he called the "fatal 19th," but a look at some of the work he did even before then shows that he never took the mandate of neutrality quite as seriously as Aitken did. Some of his earliest articles, in fact, were only barely disguised allegorical commentaries on the conflict. In an early article entitled "Observations on the Military Character of Ants," the author "Curioso" (Paine) explored the peculiar social interactions between Red and Brown ants (i.e., "redcoats" and colonials). The brown ants, he noted, were the frequent victims of the more warlike red ants who stole their food and generally bullied them around the author's backyard. Curioso warned that the brown ants must overcome their peaceful instincts and take steps to defend their territory, or face the eventual extinction of their species.

In another article that condemned the adverse health effects of Asiatic tea, "The Philanthropist" (again, Paine) recommended adopting the more salubrious home grown varieties. Asiatic teas were the most famous monopoly of the East India Company and carried the hated tea tax while indigenous teas did not. Although innocent of political partisanship on the face of it, the article was a clear endorsement of the non-importation policies the colonists had adopted as part of their campaign of resistance.

After April 19, Paine, and apparently Aitken, felt freer to become even more overt in the magazine's support of the American cause. Perhaps Paine's most material contribution to the conflict before he wrote *Common Sense* was a series of articles he co-authored instructing private citizens on the best method of producing saltpeter, an essential and chronically scarce ingredient in gunpowder.

That Paine was so successful in communicating with a common audience and holding their interest on a broad array of subjects is not surprising. From Lewes to London to Philadelphia, these were the people he had always gravitated toward and among whom he had felt so comfortable exchanging ideas in conversation. But his experience at *Pennsylvania Magazine* should not be underestimated in its importance on Paine's development as a writer with an exceptional insight into the mind and passions of his audience. The fact that he worked so hard to develop a strong rapport with the magazine's readership probably stemmed from the fact that he was not just a contributor but also a partner in the venture. Typically, while the writer worries most about the best way to say what he has to say, the publisher/editor thinks most about how to form an enduring connection with as wide an audience as possible. The success of *Pennsylvania Magazine* while Paine was there is a testament to how well he achieved both objectives. By the time his short but busy career at the magazine came to an end, Paine had honed a unique, and uniquely effective, voice: progressive but also pragmatic, intelligent but not erudite, powerful without being baroque. Above all, as a friend would later say, he had developed "a wonderful talent of writing to the tempers and feelings of the public."

During his first months in Philadelphia, as he had in London and Lewes, Paine formed a group of acquaintances and friends who shared his intellectual and political interests. Benjamin Rush was a prominent young physician and professor when he briefly met Thomas Paine browsing among the shelves of Robert Aitken's bookstore. A short time later, Rush read with great approval an anti-slavery article written by Paine in the March '75 issue of *Pennsylvania Magazine*. Paine had written on several occasions of the evils of the slave trade and was not afraid to be openly critical of his new countrymen, even those whose political principles he shared. He condemned the hypocrisy of those patriots who "complain so loudly of attempts to enslave them, while they hold so many hundred thousand in slavery." Dr. Rush, himself, had written an article against slavery, and his unpopular stance had lost him friends and patients. Recognizing the danger of expressing such sentiments publicly, Rush was struck by Paine's fearlessness, eloquence, and passion. Remembering their earlier encounter, Rush sought to become better acquainted with the author.

Notwithstanding Dr. Rush's temperance and devout piety, the two men found much that they shared in common. In addition to their aversion to slavery, both men showed an avid interest in politics, especially the escalating conflict between the Crown and the colonies. Their friendship must have begun soon after the battles of Lexington and Concord; for, Paine seems by then to have adopted his belief in the necessity for a break with Britain. As Rush would remember:

> Our subjects of conversation were political. I perceived
> with pleasure that he had realized the independence of

the American colonies upon Great Britain, and that he considered the measure as necessary to bring the war to a speedy and successful issue.

Rush was also a supporter of American independence, but he and Paine and a small circle of their acquaintances were a distinct minority. Rush observed: "When the subject of American independence began to be agitated in conversation, I observed the public mind to be loaded with an immense mass of prejudice and error relative to it."

Paine and Rush discussed the need for a new addition to the debate on the issue. Rush had taken a pass at such a pamphlet but confessed that he had "hesitated" to publish it. One factor contributing to his reluctance to publish work on independence was the personal repercussions he had experienced due to his piece on slavery. In 1775, Rush was still struggling to establish his medical practice and did not want to lose any more business because of his political beliefs. Even more so than abolition, the cause of independence was a divisive and unpopular one, and Rush "shuddered at the prospect of the consequence of its not being well received." In making the suggestion to Paine, Rush reasoned that Paine had less to lose should the pamphlet meet with disfavor. Rush had family and friends in Philadelphia, a position at the university, as well as the emerging medical practice. By the same token, however, it could be argued that these connections would have rendered him far more able to withstand the blast of public disapproval than the recent immigrant Paine. Nonetheless, whether he simply did not see the potential danger or chose to ignore it, Paine "seized upon the idea with avidity."

Perhaps to mitigate the risks the author of the proposed piece would be courting in the loyalist city, Rush counseled caution in Paine's treatment of the issue. He recommended that Paine not so much advocate independence, per se, but merely throw some light on the subject and dispel the irrational fears that attended the idea in the minds of many of their fellow citizens. Specifically, he warned that "there were two words which he should avoid by every means as necessary to his own safety and that of the public—*independence* and *republicanism*." Technically an American for barely a year, Paine ignored this advice, accepted the challenge, and pursued the project with passion, originality, and audacity.

4

A WAR OF WORDS

To disabuse the public of the "mass of prejudice and error" that prevented them from seeing the necessity of America's independence, Thomas Paine and Benjamin Rush realized that something new was required in the debate, something that went "beyond the ordinary short and cold addresses of newspaper publications . . . a work of such length as would obviate all the objections to [independence]." At first, Paine planned to write a series of three letters exploring different aspects of the independence debate and publish them in the local press. Sometime soon after he commenced work on the project, he settled instead on the publication of a single, stand-alone pamphlet.

The pamphlet was the most important and most effective medium of political advocacy in America during the eighteenth century. To be sure, there were also newspapers, broadsides, and almanacs that were popular throughout the colonies, but the pamphlet surpassed them all as an instrument of public discourse. It was in pamphlets that "the best thought of the day expressed itself" and in pamphlets that "the basic elements of American political thought of the Revolutionary period appeared first." Unlike a newspaper, the pamphlet was not intended to be discarded daily or weekly and replaced with a new issue. They were preserved, read aloud, and shared between friends and relations—sometimes over great distances. As a result, pamphlets had a better chance of carrying a lasting impact, becoming the artifacts of the debates with which they were concerned. Pamphlets were argued over in public places, advertised, excerpted, and debated in newspapers and, of course, supported and refuted by subsequent pamphlets.

The physical characteristics of the pamphlet played a great part in its utility as a medium of public debate. Pamphlets of the period were simply constructed out of a number of sheets that were printed, folded, and then loosely stitched together along the spine. The format was flexible enough to accommodate either a bauble of four pages or a tome approaching 200 pages. Such a modest method of production also meant that pamphlets were cheap, costing in most cases only a shilling or two. At 46 pages, *Common Sense* fell within the average range of pamphlets of the day—though Paine complained that the two-shilling price of the first printing was too high and lowered it for the subsequent editions he oversaw. Above all, the simplicity of its construction meant that a popular pamphlet could be printed, bound, and distributed quickly and easily to keep up with the pace of demand. In the case of the extraordinary and immediate appetite for *Common Sense*, within five weeks of its initial publication it was already into a third printing in Philadelphia alone.

Pamphlets were also extremely varied in content. It was not uncommon to find, in addition to those containing political works, pamphlets featuring poetry, scientific treatises, popular sermons, reprints of newspaper columns, even collections of correspondence. But for all the diversity of eighteenth-century American pamphlets, the majority of them fell into one of two main categories, described by Bernard Bailyn. The largest group were " . . . responses to the great events of the time," touched off by acts of parliamentary excess as well as by instances of colonial reaction such as the Boston Tea Party and the call for the first Continental Congress. The second type were "chain-reacting personal polemics: strings of individual exchanges—arguments, replies, rebuttals and counter rebuttals—in which may be found heated personifications of the larger struggle." When Paine first began to compose *Common Sense*, he intended to write a pamphlet that lay outside of both of these descriptions— neither a response to a particular event nor a reply to a previous author. Paine wanted simply to write a freestanding monograph on the subject of independence.

Given the central place occupied by the pamphlet in the period, it is not surprising that the most influential spokesman for the colonial position before *Common Sense* was another pamphleteer. In fact, John Dickinson's *Letters of a Pennsylvania Farmer* were the bestselling and most widely read pamphlets in American history—until Paine's publication. The *Letters* were widely praised for their succinct and compelling statement of colonial opposition to British colonial policy. Consequently, one of the best ways to understand the desire for reconciliation that predominated in the colonies until 1776 is to examine the arguments contained in the *Letters*. The fourteen *Letters* were published within the span of a few months from 1767–68 and were the work of the same man who would later lead the opposition in the Continental Congress to John Adams' independence faction. A wealthy, sophisticated lawyer styling himself a "farmer," Dickinson, aimed no doubt at portraying himself as a spokesman for the average colonist. His "commonness," however, went no further than the title. Dickinson spoke as and on behalf of the colonial elite. The people would have to wait until *Common Sense* for an authentic spokesman, but in 1768 it was Dickinson who led the attack against British tyranny on behalf of the beleaguered colonies. After first appearing in the *Pennsylvania Chronicle*, the letters were soon brought out in pamphlet form and gained popularity in both

America and England where they were encouraged by no less an American patriot than Benjamin Franklin.

Dickinson's views did not change much between 1768, when he was the leading opponent of British policies, and 1775, when he was the leading loyalist in the Continental Congress. It was more that the political situation deteriorated. The *Letters* were written to protest Parliament's implementation of the Townshend Acts—a series of duties levied upon American trade for the purpose of raising revenue for the crown. In the view of Dickinson and all colonists, the British government had every right to regulate American trade and to reap whatever profit they could from the mercantilist arrangement that trade was based upon. Mercantilism, in the colonial context, was understood as a relationship in which the Americans supplied British manufacturers with the raw materials needed to produce their finished goods, which were then sold back to the colonists and throughout the world.

To keep this unbalanced situation balanced, the colonies abided a series of restrictions on their own trade and manufacturing. Colonists had to buy the manufactured goods they needed from British sources. They could neither buy them elsewhere nor produce them on their own. In addition, the colonists could not sell their own raw goods on the open market but had to find the best price they could from British buyers. Unfair as these measures may seem, the colonists had grown accustomed to this arrangement. They had learned how to make a reasonable profit within it and did not begrudge the British the advantage they received as a consequence.

What the Townshend Acts represented—and what the *Pennsylvania Farmer* was determined to resist—was the intention of further burdening the colonists under taxes levied not to maintain the balance of trade but for the sole purpose of raising revenue. Dickinson was willing to concede much. In the second *Letter* he strongly affirmed Parliament's right to "regulate the trade of Great

Britain and all her colonies." He also conceded the legitimacy of all previous measures that were "calculated to regulate trade and preserve or promote a mutually beneficial intercourse between the several constituent parts of the empire." The distinction he drew between these regulations and the egregious, innovative Townshend Acts was that, while they all had the effect of taxing the colonies, the former raised revenue only incidental to the primary goal of promoting "the general welfare" while the latter were formulated solely "for the purpose of raising a revenue." As such, the new acts were not only "destructive to the liberty of these colonies," but also "unconstitutional." The distinction, while valid, is at the end of the day a bit of a fine point. Dickinson's line of argument did become the prevailing opinion of American patriots and, to an extent, solidified their opposition to Great Britain. That said, it is hard to imagine a Continental soldier stamping his frost-bitten stocking feet along a snow-covered road in eastern New Jersey, driving himself onward by reciting a passage from the *Letters of a Pennsylvania Farmer*.

Dickinson's view of the conflict was the most famous, but it was in no sense remarkable for the day. He was representative of colonial thought when he rose above the specific issue under discussion and described the fundamental worldview that underlay his argument and the thinking of his countrymen:

> We are but parts of a whole, and therefore there must exist a power somewhere to preside, and preserve the connexion . . . . This power is lodged in the parliament; and we are as much dependent on Great Britain as a perfectly free people can be.

Countless lesser-known colonial pamphlets mirrored the Farmer's penchant for using British law to condemn British behavior, reaffirming their affection for the one by placing it in opposition to the injustice of the other. It was a kind of political instance of "love the sinner, hate the sin." The titles of many of these pamphlets show their commonality on this point. There were *assertions* and *examinations* of the "The Rights of the British Colonies" as well as *considerations* of the "Propriety of Imposing Taxes in the British Colonies"— that is, the colonists' "rights" as provided in the constitution and the "propriety" within British law of certain types of taxation. It was as if, absent the protections of the British Constitution, the colonies lacked a basis for even criticizing the way they were being treated. This catch-22 presented a persistent obstacle in the path of independence. By using the British system of law to criticize British colonial policies, they were challenging British authority and reaffirming it at the same time. As a result, the state of the conflict in 1775 was essentially the same as it had been ten years earlier, with the colonists asserting their rights and George III and Parliament asserting theirs. The British had no reason to compromise, and the Americans had no real hope of recourse.

At the root of this uneasy equilibrium was the traditional view, not seriously challenged at the time, of established government as the ultimate source of all rights, law, and justice. This was the view of the colonists as well as their leaders. It was publicly articulated in the *Letters of a Pennsylvania Farmer*, and it was codified as the official view of the united colonies, in war and in peace, in the *Declaration* of July 6, 1775. Had this view remained in force, it is difficult to see how the war, which had begun on April 19, 1775, could ever have amounted to anything more than an inconclusive military extension of the political and legal gridlock between Britain and the colonies.

But a compelling new view of the relationship between the governed and their government was soon to be introduced. This view would fundamentally change the nature of the struggle from a conflict over civil rights to a war of independence. This new view held that man possessed certain inherent rights simply by virtue of his humanity; that governments were merely social constructions, created for the purpose of safeguarding those rights; and that should a government fail to protect those rights, let alone become the source of the threat against them, then that government had forfeited its claim to the title and had utterly undone *itself*.

By beginning *Common Sense* with the assertion that: "Some writers have so confounded society with government as to leave little or no distinction between them; whereas they are not only different, but have different origins . . ." and that "government even in its best state is but a necessary evil," Thomas Paine not only escalated the existing debate, but also called for a wholesale revision of the assumptions upon which that debate had been based.

"A KIND OF TREASON"

I t is hard to be certain what kind of pamphlet Benjamin Rush intended when he suggested that Paine avoid using the word *independence*, but it is safe to say that *Common Sense* fell well outside of his expectations. The cagey Ben Franklin, who returned to Philadelphia in May of 1775, may have had a better idea of what he was asking (and of what Paine would provide) when he approached Paine in October of that year to write a history of the conflict between Britain and America. The two men had, after all, traveled in the same Whig circles in London, and Franklin was well aware of the radical perspective that Paine would bring to such a project.

Political writing in London went way beyond the measured decorum and deference that characterized its American counterpart during the period. The writings of men like Wilkes and Priestley, as well as others, did not so much take issue with individual policies as condemn English government in general as riddled with corruption and decay. Their style was not one of legalistic constitutional debate but of impassioned, almost violent, declamation against the institutions, and occasionally the individuals, they saw as abetting and embodying that decay. Wilkes, for example, in his popular paper the *North Briton*, was so unrelenting in his attacks on Lord Bute, George

III's cherished friend and advisor, that Bute eventually quit the government in disgrace.

Franklin not only understood the perspective from which Paine would describe the conflict, but he also seemed to encourage it. In fact, as Paine later recalled, Franklin "proposed giving me such materials as were in his hands, towards compleating a history of the present transaction." Among those "materials" were the writings of Priestley and other radical English writers. By the time Franklin suggested his "history" project, Paine had already begun work, having "formed the outlines of *Common Sense*, and finished nearly the first part." He hoped to surprise Franklin by combining the two projects and completing the pamphlet in time for the New Year.

As Paine settled down to the project in October of 1775, the looming question was how such a new view of the Anglo-American conflict would be received. As Paine, himself, described the national mood, colonial resentment of certain British policies ran high, but "their attachment to Britain was obstinate, and it was, at that time, a kind of treason to speak against it." While the ideas of English radical writers had found some popularity among a small group of Americans, the vast majority shared the view of another Englishman, Edmund Burke, who asserted that reconciliation was in America's interest because "English privileges have made it all that it is; English privileges alone will make it all it can be." Whatever their complaints against the policies of this specific king and Parliament, writes Bernard Bailyn in his *Ordeal of Thomas Hutchinson*, no American before the publication of *Common Sense*, "was prepared to deny the structural beauties of the King-in-Parliament as a governing body." Indeed, the climate in the colonies as Paine first put pen to paper seemed, on the face of it, anything but opportune for the kind of pamphlet Paine would write.

Paine lived at that time in several rooms he rented above his former partner Robert Aitken's bookshop on Front Street. While a portion of *Common Sense* was no doubt written in these rooms, Paine also liked to write and think in public amid the commotion and clatter of taverns and coffee houses. Paine's most likely haunt was the popular London Coffee House directly across from his lodgings in Front Street, but it could have been Jonathan's or Bondford's or any of a number of similar establishments that dotted the streets and avenues closest to the city's wharf.

The coffee house was a unique and important feature of colonial towns but nowhere more so than of Philadelphia, with its constant influx of exotic coffees, busy people, and idle gossip. Bustling throughout the day, these houses seem to have been busiest at night, when people gathered to exchange the news of the day. As centers of social life, coffee houses were the ideal place for public announcements, sales, and auctions. Although horses, livestock, and trade goods were the usual items offered for sale, the following letter shows the offerings could be much larger:

> . . . upon a full consideration of the complicated affairs of the Cutter *Revenge*, it has been thought proper, and so it is determined by Congress, that the Vessel, with her guns, apparel, &c., shall be sold at public auction. And the Marine Committee has directed that the sale shall be made at the Coffee House, next Wednesday evening.

The coffee house was the logical place to conduct such a sale because it offered the largest and most diverse audience. (The coffee house mentioned by the Marine Committee was probably Paine's London since it was especially popular with sea captains.) But what surely drew Paine to his coffee house of choice was its role as a venue for topical discussion, disputation, and argument. Many of the pressing issues that occupied the minds of Philadelphians found their fullest airing between the walls of the city's coffee houses, and it is no surprise that a frequent subject of discussion during that time was politics. And because Philadelphia was the seat of the Continental Congress, when the "Chatt of the Coffee house" turned political, it was often of national rather than merely local import. In fact, as Massachusetts delegate Elbridge Gerry would attest, it was often the case that " . . . the Facts are as well known at the Coffee House of the City as in Congress." These establishments were not only the proving ground of new ideas but also the single best place for any observer and would-be agitator to gauge the general mind and mood of the widest possible cross-section of the people.

While it is impossible to guess how much, if any, of *Common Sense* was actually written in the London or any of the city's other coffee houses, one can imagine the rare opportunity such places would have afforded the pamphleteer. It is quite likely that Paine's keen grasp of the mind and mood of such a wide cross-section of colonial society was honed amid their din and clamor. Of course he would have heard much discussion on the greatest question of the day—independence. What's more, as an astute listener, he would have gathered both sides of the debate; not just the "tolerable sum-mery of arguments" in favor of separation, but, more importantly, an equally good synopsis of the Tory position.

As temporary residents often occupying humble rented lodgings or even rooms in boarding houses, many of the delegates to the Continental Congress would frequent a favorite coffee house in the evening after the day's business was done. Upon occasion, the city's coffee shops would even serve as a meeting place for the members of a congressional committee seeking refuge from the noise of the state house. The coffee house attracted a diverse mix of clientele, from common laborers and artisans to, in the words of Connecticut dele-gate Silas Deane, "Gentlemen of the first Character in this province." They were also frequently a first stop for temporary visitors—tourists, travelers, and men of business from all over the colonies. It is easy to imagine the illustrious veteran of the Headstrong Club spending his spare hours in such an atmosphere: energized, engaged, and inspired by the diversity of opinions and opinion holders.

Whether in the midst of all the gossip, jokes, and politics of the London or Bondford's or in the quiet of his rooms, Paine found that progress on *Common Sense* came slowly and arduously. For all the natural ease of his best writing, he always found the task a difficult one that required great care and patience. At several intervals he showed the work in progress to Benjamin Rush who approved—apparently in spite of the many unapologetic references to both *independence* and *republicanism*.

When the piece was judged by its author to be finished, Rush suggested they show it to a few men who were already friendly to the argument it supported. He chose Samuel Adams, Franklin, and David Rittenhouse, a Philadelphia scientist, astronomer, and inventor and perhaps the one man in North America who rivaled Franklin in the depth of his knowledge and the breadth of his accomplishments. They recommended little in the way of alterations to what Paine had written. What the four men thought of the work from a political standpoint is not known, but they must have realized the stark departure *Common Sense* was from the style and substance of the debate up to that moment. Samuel Adams may have recognized the incendiary potential of the pamphlet when he sent one of the first copies up to his acquaintances in Boston. In spite of the fact that he was among the most radical independents in Congress and would later praise *Common Sense* unreservedly, Adams seemed hesitant, at first, to show any hint of sharing the author's bold sentiments. He wrote to his friend James Warren:

I have Sent to Mrs Adams a Pamphlet which made its first Appearance a few days ago. It has fretted some folks here more than a little. I recommend it to your Perusal

and wish you would borrow it of her. Dont be displeasd
with me if you find the Spirit of it totally repugnant with
your Ideas of Government. Read it without Prejudice and
give me your impartial Sentiments of it when you may be
at Leisure.

This is not exactly a spirited endorsement from the Massachusetts
firebrand, but Adams was not alone in his response. In the days and
weeks to follow, Common Sense would "fret" many more people,
including more than a few of his colleagues in Congress. But, apart
from revealing Samuel Adams' hesitancy toward publicly embracing
the pamphlet's ideas, his letter betrays little foresight into the sudden, decisive impact it would have on the affairs of his country.

It is doubtful that even Thomas Paine had any inkling of the
overwhelming effect his efforts would produce—and he was acutely
aware of the prevailing colonial sentiments on the subject.
"Independence," he would recall in the third Crisis letter, "was a doctrine scarce and rare even toward the conclusion of the year
Seventy-five: All our politics had been founded on the hope or
expectation of making the matter up." Indeed there was little indication that the climate was at all seasonable for the ideas he would
lay before the public in the first few days of 1776. It would have been
plausible to suggest that his pamphlet was coming before the time
was ripe. Maybe the people were not yet ready to see the case so
boldly stated. After all, not even the most ardent Whig had yet dared
to call publicly for independence from Great Britain.

On the other hand, however, it would have also been possible
that Common Sense was coming too late. As one historian has posed
it, "During the fall of 1775 American Opinion appeared to be turning away from the idea of independence. Many men of judgment,
friendly to the patriot cause, thought the colonies had gone too far
in their resistance." There were concrete indications that momen-

tum had already shifted back in favor of reconciliation. In the closing months of 1775, the legislatures of Pennsylvania, New York, New Jersey, Delaware, and South Carolina had all given their delegates in Philadelphia unambiguous instructions not to vote in favor of independence. The Maryland delegation was given similar orders in January of 1776. The formidable Tory delegate Joseph Galloway gloated shamelessly over the apparent return of the pendulum: "The Tories (as they are called) make it a Point to visit the Coffee House dayly & maintain their Ground—while the violent Independents are less bold & insolent, as their Adherents are greatly diminished."

It has been often said that what set *Common Sense* apart from other voices in the debate was the passion and urgency, even anger, with which it was written. While these factors were critical aspects of Paine's approach, by themselves they would have fallen far short of Paine's objective. If he had merely written a more urgent, angry, and passionate version of the arguments contained in *Letters of a Pennsylvania Farmer*, it is unlikely there would have been much of an impact. Paine seemed to recognize from the outset that something more would be needed to turn the tide. He believed that while the moderates' arguments against separation were varied and stubbornly held, the fundamental assumptions upon which those arguments were based were eminently vulnerable.

While the word *radical* today conjures up visions of street-protests, Molotov cocktails, and extremism, it actually derives from the Latin word *radix* or "root." The extraordinary success of *Common Sense* was a direct consequence of its author setting out to write a truly *radical* work, attacking not the individual tenets of reconciliation thought, but the ideological infrastructure upon which these tenets rested. Paine announced the target of his argument in the very first sentence, "a long habit of not thinking a thing *wrong*, gives it a superficial appearance of being *right* . . . ." He was telling his audience that he would not be trying to sway their minds one way or another on the nuances of constitutional law or the details of their colonial charters that had preoccupied the debate up to that date. He was signaling his intention of speaking directly to those long-held assumptions, which they had always taken for granted.

The first assumption that Paine would attempt to dispel was perhaps the most deeply held and central to the reconciliation mind-set: the dominant view that individual and collective rights derived from government and could be preserved only by government institutions. The view of their rights as *civil* rights was so generally held as to be unquestioned among the American people, their intellectuals, or their leaders. Rather than argue directly against this view, Paine began *Common Sense* with an audacious attempt to tunnel under its foundation by declaring that the line between society and government had been blurred by writers on both sides of the debate over independence. Paine may have shrewdly discerned that this was the only way to get his audience to approach the merits of his forthcoming argument with fresh eyes, but it also echoed his ingrained belief in the existence of natural laws governing the operation of all phenomena, politics not excepted. In true Newtonian form, Paine insisted that the question was not one of *civil* but of older, more elemental *natural* rights. Any discussion of civil law was always prejudiced in favor of the established government whose province was the formulation and definition of those laws. By asserting the preeminence of natural rights over civil rights, Paine had, in effect, nullified the strongest aspects of his opponents' argument in just the first three pages of his pamphlet. By knocking even the most venerable government institutions off their privileged perch as the origin and protector of civil rights and by forcing their supporters into the less advantageous position of having to defend their record vis-à-vis the people's natural rights, Paine created an entirely new context in which to view the rest of his argument.

The shrewdest political observer of the age, Edmund Burke seemed to foreshadow Paine's reasoning when, less than a year before *Common Sense* was published, he warned Parliament:

> . . . let it be once understood [by the Americans] that your government may be one thing and their privileges another, that these two things may exist without any mutual relation—the cement is gone, the cohesion is loosened, and everything hastens to decay and dissolution.

While it is unlikely that Paine had ever heard or read an account of this speech, he obviously understood fully the danger that Burke was alluding to and the opportunity it offered to one promoting the cause of independence. While he would aim stinging barbs and devastating accusations against George III and his government, Paine's ultimate focus in doing so was to attack the "cement" and "cohesion" that held the two peoples together. Paine successfully overturned the prevailing tenets of the moderate, Tory position that "[the colonists'] rights were rooted in the ancient constitution" and that "their interests were protected by the traditional connection to Britain." Paine allowed that, while there may have been a time when American dependence on England had been beneficial, such time had long since passed, hastened not only by English tyranny but also by America's growing maturity as a nation and as a people. "Nothing can be more fallacious than this kind of argument," he said of the case for continued dependence. "We may as well believe that because a child has thrived upon milk, that it is never to have meat . . . ."

Only after the distinction between government versus society and civil rights versus natural rights was fully delineated could the formidable evidence in favor of independence begin to take hold. John Adams would later complain that most of the ideas contained in *Common Sense* were "a tolerable summary of the arguments which

I had been repeating again and again in Congress for nine months." The fact that many of Paine's arguments had already been expressed in one way or another by Adams and others enhances rather than diminishes the scope of his achievement. The essential truth is that, before *Common Sense*, these points had been put forth to little or no effect. Adams, himself, had attempted to make the case before the public in a series of letters he wrote under the pseudonym "Novanglus" (i.e., "The New Englander"). To read them is to understand why they could never have yielded the effect that *Common Sense* did. They were for the most part a halfhearted retread of the established thinking on the subject, containing neither the passion and boldness of Adams' utterances in Congress nor the candor and vision he expressed in many of his private writings. When addressing the general public in print, Adams—and all other writers prior to *Common Sense*—was competent, often eloquent, in voicing the basic rationale for separation but always stopped short of actually advocating and defending the cause of American independence. As Benjamin Rush observed, the ideas upon which Paine drew lay "like stones in a field, useless 'till collected and arranged in a building."

By insisting that people's rights were natural rights conferred not by governments but by the Creator, Paine set the context for his criticism of how well American rights and privileges had been protected by the British government. This new perspective meant that instead of the colonists having to defend their rights, it was Britain who had to defend its record of protecting and preserving those rights on behalf of its subjects. By shifting the underlying premise of the debate in this way and putting the Tory position for the first time on the defensive, Paine was free to move onto offense. Accordingly his focus shifted to the real villain of *Common Sense*—the "sullen tempered Pharaoh of England."

As the author of the shamelessly patriotic panegyric on the death of General Wolfe, Paine, the publicist, was well aware of the power of national mythology in providing a patina of legitimacy and righteousness to even the most corrupt ruler. Alternating between humor and contempt, he peeled away the layers of propaganda, pomp, and circumstance that had kept monarchs above scrutiny for so long. At the same time, Paine gradually narrowed the scope of his indictment from the general principle of hereditary rule to the English monarchy in particular to King George III in person. In one of his most famous comments on the absurdity of hereditary rule, Paine observed that, since the ability to govern was rarely passed down from one generation to the next, neither should the right to govern be passed down from parent to child. Nature, itself, mocked the practice, he suggested, by so often giving mankind "an *ass* for a *lion*."

In addition to attacking the "paltry rascally origin" of British kings, Paine found little to admire in the form of constitutional monarchy by which England had been ruled since the Glorious Revolution of 1688. Rather than an ideal hybrid of monarchical and representative government, as its defenders described it, the English system was, in Paine's view, simply " . . . the base remains to two ancient tyrannies, compounded with some new republican materials"—that is, "the remains of monarchial tyranny in the person of the king . . . the remains of aristocratical tyranny in the persons of the peers" and "the new republican materials, in the persons of the commons." For Paine the first two of these, the king and the House of Lords, because they were both hereditary, represented their own interests rather than that of those people. It was, therefore, only the House of Commons "on whose virtue depends the freedom of England." He summarized that this balance of power was actually no balance at all since the combination of the king and the lords would always trump the representatives of the people.

It is easy to see the influence of Paine's bitter experience in the excise officer's case in this portrayal of England's legislative process. But to understand the full importance of this argument one must remember that the fondest hope of many Americans who favored reconciliation was the adaptation of the King-in-Parliament system to the colonies. Some favored substituting their local colonial assemblies for the House of Commons, while others advocated the election of colonial representatives to represent them back in London. A few, as a surprised John Adams reported, even put forth the idea of a "North American Monarchy," complete with a "Continental King," a "Continental House of Lords" and a "Continental House of Commons." Whatever their stripe, these people must have winced as they saw the cow of constitutional monarchy being so savagely gored before a rapt audience.

The most singular—and to many the most shocking—characteristic of *Common Sense* was its vehement personal attack on the figure of the "crowned ruffian," King George III. Until *Common Sense* singled out the King as the chief architect and villain of British policy toward the colonies, American writers had spared George III from the brunt of their criticism even after the war had begun. It is remarkable the extent to which the colonists themselves had perpetuated the fiction that their only quarrel had been with the parliament and the colonial ministers, "our ministerial enemies," rather than the king himself. This refusal to acknowledge the king's complicity in British policy and actions toward the colonies was as pervasive as it was resilient. Americans considered the British forces sent by the king across the Atlantic to quash their rebellion to be the "Ministerial fleet & army," led by "Ministerial officers." Even Thomas Jefferson, as late as 1775, denounced the depredations of the "Ministerial forces" without casting blame on the king in whose name they marched. By attacking the king personally, Paine would be the first to focus responsibility for British policies where it belonged: squarely on the shoulders of George III. In doing so he hoped to shatter forever the colonists' image of the king as their benevolent father and the protector of their rights and liberties. But

Common Sense did not stop there. Paine also insisted that the king's conduct toward the colonies was a perversion of the expected conduct of a parent toward its children, citing the bloodshed at Lexington and Concord to condemn "the wretch, that with the pretended title of FATHER OF HIS PEOPLE can unfeelingly hear of their slaughter, and composedly sleep with their blood upon his soul." The effect was sudden and startling. After the publication of *Common Sense*, talk of the "Ministerial Army" was replaced almost overnight with talk of the "King's Troops." The king's arms were removed from their place of honor and publicly burnt by patriotic mobs. Outside Boston, George Washington ceased his habit of toasting the king at supper. Borrowing a description of George III directly from *Common Sense*, one delegate wrote home predicting that "the statue of the *Royal Brute* now standing in Bowling Green [New York] will soon be demolished." Less than two months later, it was.

Paine's attack on the king received its most significant echo in the Declaration of Independence. Jefferson, himself, had favored reconciliation as late as 1775 and had written of British troops as "Ministerial forces." But, by the time he undertook the great task of expressing the colonies' determination to form a separate and equal nation, he too had shifted the burden of blame onto George III. He charged that "the history of the present King of Great Britain is a history of repeated injuries and usurpations," and proceeded to recite a litany of those injuries, 27 of them, all beginning with the same word: "He . . . ." This shift of public odium to the person of the king had the effect of obliterating the strongest remaining bond between America and Great Britain. Americans had long believed that they could throw off the authority of Parliament while maintaining their traditional ties of loyalty and affection with the monarch—a loyalty that had been in effect since the original colonies were established by royal charter. This belief accounted for the colonists' desire to reconcile with Great Britain along the lines of their established relationship.

From the English perspective however, the British government was, and had been since 1688, a trinity, one entity with three parts—the king, lords, and commons—indivisible and inseparable. Therefore, to declare independence from Parliament was to declare independence from the whole of the British government. This belief accounts for the British government's immoderate fear of all forms of colonial resistance and their obdurate insistence that the colonies were wholly subject to the authority of Parliament "in all cases whatsoever." It was the disconnect between these two divergent perceptions that had created the acrimonious status quo that had existed between England and the colonies for over a decade. Since England—by far the more powerful of the two—had no reason to yield its position, change would have to come from the colonies. Up to 1776 the colonists had mustered the strength and unity they needed to defy the authority of Parliament. What they were not prepared to do, however, was sever their ties to the king. *Common Sense* was written in part to convince its readers of the necessity and of the justice in taking that next fateful step—to "oppose not just the tyranny but the tyrant."

After spending the bulk of *Common Sense* in systematically undoing the "mass of superstition and prejudice" that prevented Americans from seeking independence, Paine explored some of the benefits that would result from a separation from Great Britain. The idea of America benefiting from the protection of Britain's military was backward, said Paine. He reasoned that all the American wars over the previous century—from King William's War and Queen Anne's War to the War of Jenkin's Ear and The French and Indian War—had been merely extensions of larger European wars between Britain and her continental rivals. Cutting their ties to a war-prone nation like England would, Paine asserted, enhance rather than weaken American security. (Paine was right of course, as America did not find itself at war against another European nation, except England, until the dawn of the twentieth century.)

In addition to the usual evils of war, Paine pointed out the impact of these frequent wars on America's potential as a player in international commerce: " . . . whenever a war breaks out between England and any foreign power, the trade of America goes to ruin, *because of her connection with Britain.*" In addition to avoiding these periodic disruptions, Paine suggested, American trade would receive a direct and more immediate boost from independence itself, and an end to the unfair mercantilist regulations that prevented them from buying and selling on the open market. The American goods by which Great Britain had enriched itself would always find welcome foreign markets, "while eating is the custom of Europe."

Paine also argued that the American desire for foreign military and economic aid was frustrated by the fact that European nations were reluctant to commit to the American cause such as it was. The idea of underwriting the American struggle—a struggle that would most likely end in reconciliation with England—understandably left most European nations cold. But the prospect of supporting a war of independence, undertaken with the declared intention of severing the ties between Britain and her most lucrative colonial possessions, was more attractive, especially to France who was still smarting from its recent defeat in the French and Indian War.

To those who granted all these points and yet counseled patience and restraint, Paine warned that they were shirking their duty and leaving the burden to their children. He said that if it must come to war "for God's sake, let us come to a final separation, and not leave the next generation to be cutting throats, under the violated unmeaning names of parent and child."

Having thus made the case for independence and drawn a hopeful picture of an American future separate from Great Britian, Paine placed the burden of securing that future directly upon his audience. He insisted that the time had come for them to take action in the achievement of the American liberty he had described:

I am not induced by motives of pride, party or resentment
to espouse the doctrine of separation and independence;
I am clearly, positively, and conscientiously persuaded
that it is in the true interest of this country to be so; that
every thing short of *that* is mere patchwork, that it can
afford no lasting felicity—that it is leaving the sword to
our children, and shrinking back at a time when a little
more, a little farther would have rendered this continent
the glory of the earth.

Paine's prose at times reaches the lyric power of poetry when
describing the stakes, in success or failure, of the ongoing conflict. He
used simple but powerful language and imagery to evoke a cause far
larger than taxes, tariffs, and parliamentary overreach. In declaring
and defending their separation from Great Britain, said Paine in
Common Sense, the colonies would not merely be redressing their
individual and temporal grievances; they would be securing the blessings of self-government for an entire nation and for future generations:

The sun never shone on a cause of greater worth. 'Tis not
the affair of a city, a country, a province, or a kingdom,
but of a continent . . . 'Tis not the concern of a day, a
year, or an age; posterity are virtually involved in the
contest, and will be more or less affected even to the end
of time by the proceedings now. Now is the seed-time of
continental union, faith, and honour.

And, Paine warned, the cost of failure or inaction at this critical epoch would be just as enduring:

The least fracture now will be like a name engraved with
the point of a pin on the tender rind of a young oak; the

wound will enlarge with the tree, and posterity read it in
full grown characters.

As memorable and often quoted as are Paine's earlier denunciations
of Britain, these passages—in which Paine spoke like a prophet of
manifest destiny half a century before the Monroe Doctrine was written—stand as the most striking lines in the pamphlet and, indeed, in
all the literature of the revolutionary period.

For Paine, however, the opportunity of the current crisis ultimately transcended even the founding of a new nation, rising to a
unique destiny such as had never presented itself to any people in
history. He not only called Americans to their patriotic duty, but also
summoned them to shoulder a burden on behalf of civilization. He
spoke not only to those who loved their country but also to "ye that
love mankind," insisting that the danger, uncertainty, and sacrifice
that lay ahead were worth accepting for both American liberty and
for Liberty itself:

> Every spot of the old world is overrun with oppression.
> Freedom hath been hunted round the globe. Asia and
> Africa have long expelled her. Europe regards her like a
> stranger, and England hath given her warning to depart.
> O! receive the fugitive, and prepare in time an asylum
> for mankind.

Such was the substance of Paine's attack against the government
of Great Britain. Such was the tone of his challenge to the people of
America. What would be made of that attack and that challenge in
the days, weeks, and months that followed is now a matter of historic
certainty. But at the time that *Common Sense* was first laid before the
public, neither its author nor its supporters nor detractors had any
inkling of its ultimate impact on their lives or their country.

After the author was finished and satisfied with his work, Paine and Rush faced the difficult task of finding a publisher who would undertake to set in type, print, and distribute a work containing such audacious, unpopular views. In spite of his wide connections throughout Philadelphia, Rush found the search to be difficult. Finally he found a man who was willing to run the risk—an established printer, publisher, and bookseller named Robert Bell.

Bell, another immigrant from Scotland, had been in the colonies for ten years and, according to Rush, was as "high-toned" on the subject of independence as Paine. The occasional book auctions Bell conducted were popular as much for the Scotsman's flights of wit as for the volumes on sale. The author and printer planned an ambitious first run of 1,000 copies, which would consume all the paper in Bell's warehouse. It was also agreed that Paine would assume the cost of the printing—around thirty pounds—and the release of the pamphlet was scheduled for January 9. All that remained was to name the pamphlet. Paine at first favored *Plain Truth*, perhaps in homage of Dr. Franklin who had written an earlier pamphlet of the same name. In the end, to the approval—and perhaps at the suggestion—of Benjamin Rush, he settled upon *Common Sense*. Apart from a single announcement placed in a local newspaper, *Common Sense* would sink or swim solely on the merits of its composition. As Paine would remember:

> There never was a pamphlet, since the use of letters were known, about which so little pains were taken . . . . The book was turned upon the world like an orphan, to shift for itself; no plan was formed to support it.

6

"COMMON SENSE FOR EIGHTEEN PENCE"

Any uncertainty about the commercial fate of the orphan was short-lived. In the absence of a plan, plain old good luck would play a significant role in the phenomenal success of *Common Sense* and of the ideas it contained. Paine did not intend *Common Sense* to be an example of the two most popular types of Revolutionary era pamphlet; it was neither a response to an isolated event nor a reply to a previous pamphlet. Part of its success, no doubt, arose from the fact that its timely publication and contentious style meant that it would be received as an instance of both. It would, at least in the short term, become connected with a real *event*, and it would also spark a string of responses, mostly from Tories, that would last through most of the spring. The *event*, which heightened the relevance of and fueled the appetite for *Common Sense* during its first few days, originated from a long distance.

On Tuesday, January 10, 1776, *Common Sense* was published and distributed for sale in the city's many bookshops. On the same day, Philadelphians received the text of the king's speech before the opening of the new session of Parliament—given October 26, 1775, but not received in the colonies until almost three months later. The *Pennsylvania Evening Post* for January 9, 1776, published the first account of the speech, as well as the first advertisement for a new pamphlet called *Common Sense*. Samuel Adams' own reaction neatly expresses the public sentiment toward this *event*:

> I have seen the Speech which is falsly & shamefully called most gracious. It breathes the most malevolent Spirit, . . . and determines my opinion of the Author of it as a Man of a wicked Heart . . . . What have we to expect from Britain, but Chains & Slavery?

That Thomas Paine's attack against the policies and character of George III was being circulated throughout the colonies simultaneous with the text of the king's speech was an important stroke of marketing luck. Paine recognized as much himself, writing in the appendix of the second edition of *Common Sense*:

> Had the spirit of prophecy directed the birth of this production, it could not have brought it forth at a more seasonable juncture or a more necessary time. The bloody mindedness of the [speech] shew the necessity of pursuing the doctrine of the [pamphlet].

Instead of being viewed as shockingly insubordinate, Paine's personal attack on the king was greeted as an apt response to this new provocation. Not that Paine showed any gratitude for the boost in sales—he labeled the speech "a piece of finished villainy."

Further adding to its momentum and currency, *Common Sense* also brought forth a frantic volley of respondents, some attempting to support but most to attack Paine and rebut his arguments. The response began almost immediately in the city's newspapers and by March had been taken up by a series of pamphleteers of varying abilities. This public discussion began as a flood and maintained a steady flow from the week *Common Sense* was published up until the Declaration of Independence announced the resolve of a new nation. According to historian Eric Foner, "Between January and July of 1776, scarcely a week went by without a lengthy article in the Philadelphia press attacking or defending, or extending and refining Paine's ideas, and the same was true in other cities as well." For Paine and his new publishers, this had the net effect of keeping the public mind focused on "*Common Sense* and Independence" for the remainder of winter, through spring, and into the summer of 1776.

Most of *Common Sense*'s detractors were innocuous and forgettable. Such a work was a pamphlet, coincidently named *Plain Truth*, published in March by Robert Bell but quickly dismissed by independents and Tories alike as vastly inadequate to the task of toppling *Common Sense*. So negative was the public's reaction against *Plain Truth*—including public burnings of the pamphlet and the destruction of print shops that dared print it—that the author declined to reveal himself. He remained anonymous until the twentieth century, when he was discovered to have been a Maryland loyalist named James Chalmers.

A more substantial challenge came in the form of a series of letters published in the *Pennsylvania Gazette* in April of 1776, under the penname "Cato." Their author was a prominent and wealthy Philadelphia loyalist named William Smith, also the provost of the College of Philadelphia. According to John Adams, Smith had a reputation as an able intellect without a single other redeeming quality. His critique against *Common Sense*, while sometimes cogent and well turned, often degenerated into arrogant, *ad hominem* attacks against Paine. Paine responded to his challengers, especially

"Cato," with a series of letters in the *Pennsylvania Journal* signed "The Forester." However eloquently forceful parts of "Cato"'s assault may have been, it soon became evident that a tide had changed, irrevocably and irresistibly.

The efforts of loyalist writers to counter the progress of *Common Sense* met at first with some small notice but faded rapidly as time went on, the apparent dying gasps of an idea whose time had passed. In retrospect it is astonishing how quickly this change was accomplished—that within a mere lightning flash of historical time, three or four months at most, what had been the prevailing ideology of an entire continent had become so utterly and hopelessly irrelevant. By the time the polemical smoke had cleared, according to one contemporary witness and early historian, the "Cato"s and other enemies of independence reclined in defeat and over the field that "the principles of Paine's pamphlet now stalked in triumph over the field."

The greatest external factor contributing to the singular success of the pamphlet was the fact that it was written, published, and first came to prominence in the unique, flourishing city on the Delaware River. In addition to having the largest population of any colonial city, Philadelphia also had the highest proportion of politically active citizenry. A great number of the city's artisans and tradesmen had already been accustomed to voting for their representatives in the Pennsylvania assembly and so took great interest in the political debates. The city's active press fed, and was fed by, this interest in public affairs that was widespread enough to support 27 printing presses and six newspapers. (The *Pennsylvania Evening Post* was the most frequently published, appearing three times a week.) The pace of exchange was brisk and presented the city's print shops with additional opportunities to issue pamphlets, broadsheets, and "penny numbers," which addressed especially hot topics. All of these publications found their way into the hands of the public through as many as 30 bookshops that dotted the city.

In addition to being an eager immediate audience for controversial political material like *Common Sense*, Philadelphia was an ideal launching pad toward reaching the wider American audience. In part because of its geographic position at the center of the thirteen colonies and in part because a Philadelphian, Benjamin Franklin, had overseen the creation and modernization of the colonial postal system, Philadelphia was the primary hub for the flow, not just of the mail, but also of magazines, almanacs, and pamphlets.

While the Continental Congress was in session, there was heightened interest throughout the colonies in the affairs of the city. Recent news and developments from Philadelphia were eagerly sought by readers from Boston to Charleston. The delegates themselves were only too happy to satisfy their constituents' appetite for local Philadelphia color, often enclosing local books and newspapers along with their letters home.

When *Common Sense* first hit the city's bookstalls on January 10, 1776, congressional delegates—independents, Tories, and moderates alike—were among its most avid readers. After reading and discussing *Common Sense* among themselves, delegates eagerly became self-appointed publicists and distributors for the anonymously published work. In sending copies back to their friends and families, most delegates expressed approval of the pamphlet's ideas, and many even pronounced themselves convinced by its eloquent advocacy for separation. In some cases individual delegates, not sure of their own or their addressee's views toward independence, demurred comment on the ideas it contained. In the case that pro-independence delegates were sending *Common Sense* to one whose fellow-feeling they were certain of, they openly and effusively praised both the pamphlet and its author, and welcomed it as an important, perhaps decisive addition to the ongoing discourse.

One of the first congressmen to mention *Common Sense* in his correspondence—and the first by a month to express his accord with its sentiments—was Josiah Bartlett of New Hampshire, who not only promised to send along the pamphlet, but also expressed his wish that its sentiments would have an enlightening effect on the minds of his constituents:

> Sir,   Philadelphia Jany 13th 1776.
>
> . . . This morning I see in the newspaper . . . that Portsmouth . . . is very much afraid of the idea conveyed by the frightful word Independence! This week a pamphlet on that Subject was printed here, and greedily bought up and read by all ranks of people. I shall send you one of them, which you will please to lend round to the people; perhaps on consideration there may not appear any thing so terrible in that thought as they might at first apprehend . . . .

Unlike Bartlett, other delegates in the first few weeks after its publication sent *Common Sense* home with the evident intention of using it to sound out the sentiments of their friends and constituents on the issues. On January 13, Henry Wisner of New York hurriedly scribbled the following on the title page of a copy of *Common Sense* before sending it home to a colleague:

> Sir,
>
> I have only to ask the favor of you to read this pamphlet, consulting Mr. Scott and such of the Committee of Safety as you think proper, particularly Orange and Ulster, and let me know their and your opinion of the general spirit of it. I would have wrote a letter on the subject, but the bearer is waiting.

In a similar cautious vein, Joseph Hewes of North Carolina wrote home on February 11:

> The only pamphlet that has been published here for a long time I now send you, it is a Curiosity, we have not put up any to go by the Waggon, not knowing how you might relish independency. The Author is not known. Some say Doctor Franklin had a hand in it, he denies it.

But by the middle of February, with the pamphlet already in its third printing, delegates were more likely not only to mention the effect of *Common Sense* on the public at large but also to offer their own views on its worth. Samuel Ward offered his own strong opinion and recorded the very real impact the pamphlet was having in Philadelphia and beyond:

> Dear Brother   Philadelpa. 19th Feby. 1776
>
> . . . I see no Advertisement in the Providence Paper for reprinting Common Sense; that Pamphlet ought surely to be distributed throughout all the Colonies if it was even at the public Expence. It has done immense Service; I am told by good Judges that two thirds of this City & Colony are now full in his Sentiments; in the Jerseys & Maryland &c they gain ground daily.

Josiah Bartlett was happy to report that the tenets of Paine's argument had at least begun to exert the influence he had hoped for a month earlier. On February 19 he wrote:

> The Pamphlet Common Sense has already had three Editions in this City; in the last there is an apendix and

large additions, it has also been reprinted at N. York; by the best information it has had a great Effect on the minds of many here & to the Southward.

From Watertown, Massachusetts, John Palmer wrote to his friend John Adams thanking him for sending the pamphlet—"it is very welcom"—and explaining that the only reason it had not been reprinted locally was that one of Watertown's printers had died and that the other was gravely ill.

Still some delegates bemoaned the fact that the change was not taking place even more quickly. Playing on the pamphlet's title, Oliver Wolcott accounted for any remaining resistance to the idea of independence this way: "Common Sense operates pritty well, but all Men have not common sense."

Nonetheless, the overwhelming effect, beginning in Philadelphia on January 9 and reverberating throughout the colonies in the weeks and months that followed, was one of unalloyed triumph for the philosophy of *Common Sense*. John Adams' secondhand account of developments in the southern colonies was typical of that trend:

> . . . Last Evening, a Letter was received, by a Friend of yours, from Mr John Penn, one of the Delegates from North Carolina, lately returned home to attend the Convention of that Colony, in which he informs, that he heard nothing praised in the Course of his Journey, but Common sense and Independence. That this was the Cry, throughout Virginia.

In the next few months, virtually all of Philadelphia continued to follow the battles in the city press between the Forester (Paine) and his adversaries. As with the pamphlet that started it all, permanent and temporary Philadelphia residents also shared these replies and rebuttals with their friends to the north and south. Fulfilling his promise to send everything of interest published in the city back to his wife in Braintree, John Adams sent not only the newspapers, broadsides, and pamphlets but also detailed accounts of the interested parties. In one such letter, offering background on the various personages behind the works he was sending, Adams resembled nothing so much as a color commentator at a boxing match:

> The Writer of Common Sense, and the Forrester, is the same Person. His Name is Payne, a Gentleman, about two Years ago from England, a Man- who G[eneral] Lee says has Genius in his Eyes. The Writer of Cassandra is said to be Mr. James Cannon a Tutor, in the Philadelphia Colledge. Cato is reported here to be Dr. Smith . . . one of the many irregular, and extravagant Characters of the Age.

In this way, because of the unique geographical, social, and political importance of Philadelphia, what might have remained merely a local phenomenon in any other American city was able to engage a truly national audience. Of course, all these factors combined were nothing more than latent potential. Each of the books, pamphlets, and broadsides published in the city enjoyed those same advantages. Yet nothing else came even close to the success of *Common Sense*. The single most important factor in that success was the unique genius of the pamphlet itself. And yet the unprecedented success of *Common Sense* also owed much to the unique genius of the man who wrote it. In the aftermath of its initial reception, Paine, now something of a minor celebrity, displayed what would become two of his lifelong trademarks—a talent for self-promotion and selfless commitment to a cause in which he believed.

Sometime soon after January 10, both author and publisher quickly realized that, even without the unsolicited but welcome assistance of the independents in Congress, they had at the very least a minor sensation on their hands. Plans began almost immediately for a second, revised edition and a larger printing. Barely a month after it first went on sale, the pamphlet was in its third edition with a German translation also in preparation. Unfortunately, all this success did nothing for the personal relationship between Paine and Robert Bell, a relationship which soured after a disagreement over the author's royalties. Paine had read with deep concern about the desparate conditions of the Continental army then laying siege to the city of Quebec. In spite of his own chronic penury, Paine decided to donate his entire share of the revenues generated by the success of *Common Sense* to buy winter clothing for the troops. When Captain Pryor, whom Paine had asked to oversee the purchase of the provisions, called at the Third Street shop, Bell was less than forthcoming. As a result Paine canceled plans to release an expanded second edition with Bell and took charge of the publication himself.

Paine found a new partner in William Bradford, onetime friend and rival of another Philadelphia printer—Benjamin Franklin. To meet the enormous demand, Paine and Bradford sub-contracted the services of two additional printers, Robert Towne and Stynes & List, to print a combined run of 6,000 copies. Stynes & List, who specialized in publications for Pennsylvania's large German population, was further commissioned to translate and print the German edition. In spite of the fact that the second edition would be substantially revised and expanded, Paine determined that the price would be no more than one shilling—half the cost of Bell's first printing. Paine's intention was to make *Common Sense* available to virtually anyone who had a desire to read it. He also released his copyright throughout the colonies, encouraging enterprising printers everywhere to publish their own editions of *Common Sense*. Paine's instincts throughout this period were admirably atypical. Rather than seizing the personal opportunity posed by his pamphlet's success, he instead pursued every chance to leverage that success in service of the American cause.

So pitch-perfect and commanding was the style of *Common Sense*, so suited to the time and the mood of the people, that many had a hard time believing it came from such an unheralded, unexpected figure. Even after Paine's authorship had been revealed, rumors persisted for years that *Common Sense* was the work of one of the leading men of Congress or, more exotically, that he was a veteran scribbler and provocateur from London's grub street, or even that he was the mystery shrouded "Junius"—the well-connected, anonymous writer who had attacked George III's government from the English side of the Atlantic.

More than a month after its publication, Paine was still referred to by some Philadelphians as the pamphlet's "imputed" author. Admiral Lord Howe's private secretary was moved to distraction by the insolence of what he called "Adam's Pamphlet." Even years later, John Adams, then on a diplomatic mission in Europe, found it necessary to demure that he was not the author of *Common Sense* and furthermore that the erroneous byline "*à une fameux proscrit M. Adams . . .*" must have referred to his cousin Samuel. While in time Paine would become famous on both sides of the Atlantic as the author of *Common Sense* and other works, it seemed that, in the beginning, many friends of independence found it hard to believe that such an unknown fellow had done their cause so much good. At the same time, its enemies found it hard to accept that such a man had caused them so much grief.

When he initially wrote in the pages of *Common Sense* that "Reconciliation is now a fallacious dream . . . ", Paine was speaking for himself rather than for the general public. His hope in publishing *Common Sense* was to convert a portion of public opinion to his own beliefs. The extent to which he would succeed surpassed not only his own aspirations but also all publishing precedent as well. By April of

1776, what Paine had expressed as his private belief when he sat down to write his pamphlet could accurately be described as the "common faith," representing the dominant view of Americans. They were now convinced that all the dictates of nature and reason supported a declaration of independence; that all hopes for reconciliation were naïve at best and traitorous at worst; and that all such plans, projects, and sentiments that preserved American dependence on England were now as obsolete and as useless as last year's almanac.

There were other events, in the north and south, that contributed to the frenzy with which the fire of independence spread throughout the country in the early months of 1776. People throughout the colonies were outraged when they heard of a punitive raid against the unprotected town of Falmouth, Maine. A squadron of British ships under Captain Henry Mowat, anchored in the town's harbor and commenced a bombardment, including incendiary bombs, that lasted from 9 o'clock in the morning to 6 o'clock in the evening. In the end, most of what had been a prosperous, coastal town—including 140 homes—was in ashes. In Virginia, the Royal Governor Lord Dunmore was rumored to be inciting slaves and Native Americans to attack his rebellious subjects. This speculative sin was punctuated by his very real decision to attack and burn Norfolk, at the time the largest town in the entire colony. But in and of themselves these events were little if at all different from similar depredations the colonies and Great Britain had previously endured. What had changed was the context in which these events were viewed by the colonists—a new context created mostly by the success of *Common Sense*.

"Common Sense and Independence" wrote Adams, describing the catchwords of the movement that took his countrymen by storm in the months leading up to their formal declaration of separation from England. The words were linked in the vernacular of the time because in the minds of the people they formed a single idea, an idea whose time had come. Eric Foner describes the material progress of that idea as embodied in Paine's 46 pages:

> At a time when the most widely circulated colonial news-
> papers were fortunate if they averaged two thousand sales
> per week, when the average pamphlet was printed in one
> or two editions of perhaps a few thousand copies,
> *Common Sense* went through 25 editions and reached
> literally hundreds of thousands of readers in the single
> year of 1776.

Paine, himself, felt he was well "within compass" to estimate the sales of his pamphlet in the first three months at 120,000, a num-ber that most historians accept as accurate or even low. By the end of the year, the total number of copies in circulation—authorized editions and bootlegs—would stand at 500,000. This did not include the many foreign editions, which in some cases experienced, as the American Silas Deane would write from Paris, "a greater run, if pos-sible, here than in America." Even so, there was roughly one copy of *Common Sense* for every five inhabitants of America, nearly one per every household. Add to this astonishing figure the fact that most copies were read by or to more than one person—in some cases many more—and the audience for *Common Sense* far surpasses that of any other printed work apart from the Bible. Moses Coit Taylor, who was not only a good friend to several congressmen but also a prominent literary scholar of the period, said that *Common Sense*:

> . . . was precisely fitted to the hour, to the spot, to the pas-
> sions of men. . . . It brushes away the tangles and cobwebs
> of technical debate, and flashes common sense upon the
> situation. It was meant for plain men, in desperate anger,
> and desperately in earnest.

7

"INDEPENDENCE
LIKE A TORRENT"

The Second Continental Congress convened on May 5, 1775, with two primary objectives: to formulate a unified political response to British policy and to centralize management of the growing war effort. On the political front their most notable achievements in the first few months had been the Olive Branch Petition and the Declaration of the Causes for Taking up Arms, both ratified in July of 1775. Militarily, they took steps to shore up the "Boston Army," besieging the British garrison within that city, and formed a general plan for the creation of a larger, more continental force. They elected four Major Generals, eight Brigadier Generals, and appointed George Washington commander in chief of the Continental army.

In this flurry of activity, it would have been hard, however, to determine with any exactness the larger objective or objectives being pursued. What was the difference between these latest diplomatic utterances and the ones they had ratified the year before during the First Continental Congress? And as for the newly formed army, what precisely were they fighting to achieve?

Thomas Jefferson conveyed a sense of the sharp divisions on these and most other questions in an anecdote related in his autobiography. John Dickinson, flush with "delight" after the passage of his conciliatory Declaration of Causes, couldn't help but gloat a little over his triumph. Jefferson wrote:

> The vote being passed, altho' further observation on it was out of order, [Dickinson] could not refrain from rising and expressing his satisfaction and concluded by saying "there is but one word . . . in the paper which I disapprove, & that is the word *Congress*," on which Benjamin Harrison [of Virginia] rose and said "there is but one word in the paper . . . of which I approve, and that is the word *Congress*."

And yet for all of their division there were still some points on which Mr. Dickinson and Mr. Harrison, and indeed all of the delegates, agreed. Thomas Jefferson remembered much later in his *Notes on the State of Virginia*: "It is well known, that in July of 1775, a separation from Great-Britain and the establishment of Republican government had never entered into any person's mind." Samuel Adams may have been the exception that proved the rule, but Jefferson was essentially accurate. In the subsequent months, however, a small but determined group of New England and Virginia delegates began to privately support and quietly advocate, if not Republican government then at least independence from Great Britain. As they became more confident, they began to pursue indirect means of turning the tide in their favor. Both their intentions and their tactics, however, were decried by the majority of their colleagues. Some delegates who opposed them did so out of a strong attachment to the British system under which they had prospered, others from the knowledge their constituents wanted no part of independence.

According to John Adams, the Congress was divided into one-third Tories, one-third moderates who favored taking a harder line against Parliament but stopped well shy of desiring independence, and one-third "true blue" independence men. Adams himself was the floor leader of the pro-independence faction, which included most of the New England delegates and a few Virginians such as the fiery Richard Henry Lee and the reserved, brilliant Thomas Jefferson. Dickinson was not only the leading Tory but also the de facto leader of Congress since it had convened in May.

In order to strengthen their position, Adams' group needed to appeal to the middle faction, the "timid" third as he called them. Unfortunately, rather than winning some of the moderates over to their way of thinking, the first tentative steps of the independents had the opposite effect. In November 1775 the Congress voted in favor of a resolution to formally reaffirm the colonists' loyalty to the British crown. In the following weeks one delegation after another was put under strict orders by their respective colonial legislatures to oppose any measure that might tend toward "independency." Many within Congress and without, men of patriotic conviction, felt in their hearts that they had already gone too far.

When John Adams left Philadelphia on December 6 to return to Braintree for the holidays, it was no doubt with a heavy heart—one full of frustration and doubt. The high hopes that he had brought with him on his first trip to the city more than a year earlier had been overcome by a sense of not only disappointment but also of fatigue and some sadness over the atmosphere of acrimony and partisan strife that had poisoned the Congress. He must have been happy, indeed, to leave that place of disaffection to return to the bosom of his family and the people he had spent his life among. By the same token, the were no doubt many in Congress—Tories and moderates alike—who were glad to see the back of Mr. Adams. The most influential and determined leader of the pro-independence wing of Congress would not return until February 9 of the New Year.

On the day before *Common Sense* was published, the Congress was in the midst of a debate over how to respond to the king's speech before Parliament, the text of which they had received the day before. James Wilson, a Pennsylvania Tory and respected legal scholar, proposed that they formally renounce the king's accusation that the colonies wanted independence. Wilson insisted that since the colonists undertook their struggle with the intention of re-establishing their rights under the constitution, they should have remained committed to that single objective. Framed in this way, these kinds of resolutions were proposed as much to rebuke the independents for their inconstancy and infidelity as to reassure the king of colonial loyalty.

Wilson's measure attracted strong support among Tories and moderates, and, in the absence of his younger cousin, Samuel Adams rose to oppose it. With the support of Benjamin Franklin and George Wythe of Virginia, he succeeded in getting a vote on Wilson's measure postponed. He suggested instead that the Congress take up the matter of Franklin's "plan of confederation," a plan that independents hoped would further erode the institutions of royal authority in the colonies. Dickinson then took the floor and, drawing up his towering, skeletal frame, called upon the delegates to defeat Adams' proposal. As they had for nearly nine months, the delegates obeyed the rigid, imposing Colonel Dickinson, who probably relished this display of his power and influence no more or less than he had countless similar shows of support on other such occasions. He had no way of knowing that it would be his last—that from the very next day, Tories, in Congress and throughout the country, would begin fighting a defensive, rear-guard action against the irresistible advance of "Common Sense and Independence."

The debut copies of *Common Sense* were put on sale at Bell's and distributed to Philadelphia bookshops on Tuesday, January 9;

they were on sale throughout the city by the next day. The first mention of the pamphlet by any members of Congress was not until Saturday January 13, in personal letters by Samuel Adams and Josiah Bartlett—both independents—and a moderate from New York, Henry Wisner. There is little doubt that by then most of the delegates of all persuasions had been exposed to *Common Sense* either directly or in discussions with colleagues, friends, and perfect strangers. The members of Congress helped spread the word of *Common Sense* back to their own colonies, but what effect did it have on their more immediate environment—on their own opinions and on the contentious equilibrium between the Tory/moderate majority and the independent minority?

In addition to reading it for themselves and discussing it with their colleagues, the delegates no doubt witnessed first-hand the enormous impression *Common Sense* was making on the people of the city. As temporary visitors, most of them lived in lodging houses such as those owned by Mrs. Sarah Yard, in which the whole Massachusetts delegation lived. As a result of their humble accommodations, and in the absence of their families, many delegates spent a healthy amount of time in public places—taverns and coffee houses. The delegates patronized many of these establishments but favored the City Tavern on Second Street and the popular London Coffee House on Front Street directly across from Paine's own lodgings. Given the role such places played as forums of public debate, it is impossible that any patron could have failed to notice the increasing popularity of the ideas that Paine had publicized.

The correspondence of the members of Congress demonstrates the direct impact *Common Sense* had on individual delegates. It redoubled the conviction of some independents, swayed the minds of many middle grounders, and in some cases even "turned Tories into Whigs." But the most important role *Common Sense* would play was in breaking the deadlock between the entrenched Tory forces and the revitalized pro-independence delegates. Declaim and hold forth as they might, the actions of each delegate were largely circumscribed by the instructions they had been given by their home colonies and the constituents who had elected and sent them to Philadelphia. Changing the position of the Continental Congress was really a matter of changing the substance of the instructions under which they served. That is why the stark instructions to oppose independence that several of the delegates had received toward the end of 1775 were so devastating to the radicals. It is also why the widespread, grassroots success of *Common Sense* proved so critical to the ultimate decision of Congress to vote in favor of independence.

John Adams returned to Philadelphia on February 8, 1776, and took his seat in Congress the next day. While passing through New York he had bought two copies of *Common Sense*, one for himself and one to send to his wife. His uneventful trip took only 15 days in spite of the heavy snows encountered on the first leg of the trip. The hours had been brightened by the companionship of his fellow Massachusetts delegate, Elbridge Gerry, but Adams could not shake entirely the sense of gloom and worry that burdened him. The challenges that had been great seemed to be mounting. In addition to the memory of the divisive state of the Congress he was returning to, he also had the knowledge of the recent disastrous defeat of the American troops beneath the walls of Quebec and the precarious state of the army at Cambridge, where Washington was losing soldiers by the hundreds as their terms of enlistment expired and they headed home.

From a personal standpoint, Adams' situation in Congress had not changed since he had left the first week of December. He was still the *bête noire* of the Tories and their moderate allies. In spite of the fact Adams and Dickinson had once been friends, they were no longer even civil to each other. Ever since a letter written by Adams in which he called Dickinson a "piddling genius" whose behavior lent a "silly cast" to the proceedings of Congress had been intercepted by the British and published in the Tory press, the proud Philadelphian refused to speak with Adams or even acknowledge him as they passed each other in the street. These, of course, were mere annoyances to Adams. Of more importance was the change he noticed in the minds of some of his more moderate delegates and, more importantly, in the wider public beyond the wall of the Pennsylvania Statehouse. He recognized this change as owing greatly to the success of Paine's pamphlet. He wrote to his wife:

> You ask, what is thought of Common sense. Sensible Men think there are some Whims, some Sophisms, some artfull Addresses to superstitious Notions, some keen attempts upon the Passions, in this Pamphlet. But all agree there is a great deal of good sense, delivered in a clear, simple, concise and nervous Style.

Adams had some reservations even then about some of Paine's notions of the kind of government that would replace imperial rule, notions he felt were "too democratical." But he recognized the effect *Common Sense* was having on the public, especially in the south. Adams had long believed that the reluctance of the southern states to countenance any movement toward separation was the principle reason for the impasse in Congress. The northern colonies were already in the pro-independence column. The middle colonies—Pennsylvania, Maryland, and New Jersey—he understood were opposed to independence for a variety of cultural, religious, and economic reasons. If a shift were going to occur it would most likely come from the south.

Sensing that events beyond their control were beginning to weaken their hold on the Congress, the Tories welcomed Adams back by launching a campaign to have him disqualified from serving as a delegate. Their almost absurd argument was that, since Adams held the office of Chief Justice in the new Massachusetts government, he was an "interested" party and, therefore, had a personal motivation to pursue independence. Adams defended himself by saying that if this were true, anyone who served under a previous government was also "interested" and inclined to oppose independence. Calling their bluff, he suggested that, by such reasoning, they could all be called "interested" parties and that all delegates should therefore take an oath that they would not seek office in any *future* government brought into being by the actions of Congress. Delegates of all persuasions realized the folly of this line of reasoning and the proposal was defeated. This type of underhanded, *ad hominem* lawmaking was not the kind of move the Tories would have tried two months earlier. It was an ill-conceived, partisan trick and an act of desperation.

Sensible to their growing momentum, the independents began to push their own agenda, such as a resolution to open American ports to trade with all nations except Great Britain. Adams and others understood that such a step would in effect be an assertion of economic independence and might set the stage for American independence itself. In previous months their attempts had been defeated. This time, however, the Tories adopted a defensive policy, avoiding a direct confrontation and seizing every opportunity to, in Adams' words, "evade, retard and delay every motion that we made."

Virginian George Wythe, the eminent legal scholar under whom Thomas Jefferson had studied, rose in support of opening the ports while acknowledging that opening the ports to foreign trade would require foreign trade agreements. Foreign trade agreements, of course, were agreements between *nations*, forcing the Congress to deal with the issue of whether they were a nation or a dependency of Great Britain. The Tories reacted by taking up every insignificant, marginal issue for debate—from considering and responding to the routine correspondence of their Generals to minutiae such as individual troop dispatches. Pro-independence delegates condemned this transparent policy of attending to frivolous busywork while matters of such great importance remained unattended to.

But while the Congress was mired in division and gridlock, the country around them was beginning to think and move in unison toward one conclusion. Josiah Bartlett's wish that *Common Sense* would convince his people of the desirability of independence would be returned tenfold. During the same weeks that *Common Sense* was making its way through the colonies—in bootleg copies, church sermons, and newspaper reprints—the independents succeeded in passing a motion to appoint a committee of five, headed by James Wilson, to explore ways of introducing the idea of independence to the people. By the time Wilson's committee delivered their 6,000-word address to the people, the people themselves had already left Wilson and the rest of the Congress behind. The document was tabled and forgotten.

"Postponement was the object of our antagonists," wrote Adams of the Tories, and he tried with little success to break the impasse. Within the Congress, *Common Sense* was having an effect to be sure. It no doubt converted some and moved others. But the real impetus would come from the people. Accustomed to looking to the Congress for guidance and leadership, they had found their own voice in the pages of *Common Sense*, and its echo would soon shake the walls of the Statehouse.

The first indication to the delegates that *Common Sense* was having as significant an impact in other cities, towns, and parishes as it was having in Philadelphia was tame enough. Reverend Samuel Cooper of Boston wrote to Benjamin Franklin, asking: "How is Common Sense relished among you? It is eagerly read and greatly admired here." Early on, there was ample reason for pro-independence delegates to take heart that at least some of the people were beginning to move in their direction:

The Pamphlet called *Common Sense* is read with great
Avidity. The Doctrine it holds up is well calculated for
the climate of N[ew] England and though some *pidling*
Souls shrink at the Idea 99 in 100 wish for a Declaration
of Independence from the Congress.

Even in some of the colonies that were not considered radical
strongholds, "*Common Sense* and Independence" were gaining
ground. From Philadelphia, one wrote of the pamphlet's anonymous
author "I am told by good Judges that two thirds of this City &
Colony are now full in his Sentiments; in the Jerseys & Maryland &c
they gain ground daily."

The independents did not have time to enjoy their rising fortune, however. Events throughout the colonies were quickening
apace. As one observer wrote "*Common Sense* . . . is read to all
ranks; and as many read, so many become converted; though perhaps the hour before were most violent against the least idea of
independence." It was not long before the delegates began to hear
from and about some of these new converts to the cause. A New
Yorker wrote proudly:

> There has been a pamphlet written and publish'd here
> against our *natural Rights* and Common Sense. It has met
> with its Demise. Some of our sturdy Sons seiz'd between
> 1500 and 2000 of them at Sam Loudon's, and consigned
> them to the flames.

A Philadelphian reported that "seven thousand men had risen in arms
in Maryland to compel their convention to declare independence."

Into an atmosphere of uncertainty and doubt *Common Sense*
had come like the revelation of an absolute truth. As Samuel Adams
would say, the people acted as if they had been "awakened" by

Common Sense—they now felt that they knew what must be done in the face of the gathering crisis. Patience was not a quality much in favor. And it was only a matter of time before they began to turn their frustration with what they saw as a lack of progress toward independence onto their leaders in Congress.

One Bostonian wrote to Philadelphia, saying of *Common Sense*: "Tis universally admired here. If the Congress should adopt the sentiments of it, it would give the greatest satisfaction to our people." Others were less polite and more direct: "People can't account for the hesitancy they observe" wrote a friend to John Adams, adding with some sarcasm that the people " . . . wonder why the principles and dictates of Common Sense have not the same Influence upon the Enlarged minds of their superiours" as on themselves.

John Adams wrote back angrily that the Congress was moving as quickly as it could. They had opened the ports and authorized privateers to harass British ships. Were not these important steps toward independence? He may well have had a point, but there was no denying the truth of the matter. As one citizen wrote to his delegate, "The People are now ahead of you . . . The People's blood is too Hot to admit of delays—All will be in confusion if independence is not declared immediately." In the words of one constituent, the people were beginning to grumble: "What in the name of *Common Sense* are you gentlemen of the Continental Congress about?"

The groundswell of pro-independence sentiment outside the Congress certainly emboldened the independents within. In addition to proposing and passing the measures to open ports and encourage privateers, the radicals pursued other measures leaning toward separation and effectively opposed efforts to return to the old cycle of obsequious petitions and groveling re-affirmations of loyalty. "The success of *Common Sense* showed the radicals that they might safely rush in where Tom Paine had not feared to tread," as historian John Miller put it. "They discovered that they could write the word 'independence' without a quaver and that a large number of Americans could bear to look upon it." The increasing popular support in the wake of *Common Sense* not only encouraged the independents to press their program more strenuously, but also influenced the way many of them thought and spoke about the conflict with Britain. It was only after reading Paine that John Adams drew up a detailed list of objectives, including near the bottom a call for a "Declaration of Independency." A stark example of the direct influence *Common Sense* had on the thought, words, and deeds of many delegates can also be seen in the proposal of George Wythe and Richard Henry Lee to insert into the privateering measure language that described the king, rather than the ministry, as "the Author of our Miseries."

As a result of an erosion of their popular support and a slow migration of some of their moderate allies away from the Tory position, the anti-independence faction, for the first time, seemed to be losing more battles than they won. Their despair was matched by the ebullience of their opponents. "Every Post and every Day," Adams exulted, "rolls in upon Us Independence like a Torrent." The tide of the great debate had indeed turned decidedly against the loyalists, and not even their leaders knew what to do, apart from try to delay and obstruct the flood as long as they could. In that effort they had one solid and perhaps immovable advantage. The delegations of a majority of colonies were prevented by their instructions to vote for independence or in some cases to support any measure that might lead to independence. The Congress's move toward independence ground to a halt on these anti-independence instructions, some of which had been issued only weeks before *Common Sense* was published. The delegates would have to return home and request new instructions freeing them to vote for independence.

In many cases, in light of the widespread popular shift in favor of "Common Sense and Independence," this would not be a difficult task—requiring only the time to make the trip. In other cases, however, it would prove more complicated. In South Carolina, delegate Christopher Gadsden provoked shock and outrage when he returned home from Congress calling for independence and brandishing a copy of *Common Sense*. But throughout April and May, one colonial assembly after another wrote and ratified new instructions allowing their delegates to cast their vote in favor of independence, should such a measure be proposed. Even Gadsden's South Carolina constituents eventually ratified similar instructions. Missing among these various permissions to go along with a declaration of independence was the authority to initiate such a measure. Then, on May 15, Virginia gave its delegates instructions to propose independence. Virginia, more than any other colony, had taken the ideas of *Common Sense* to heart and been transformed by them. Edmund Randolph, then a young man who would later represent Virginia as a congressman, was proud of the central role his people had played in those momentous times and recognized the critical influence *Common Sense* had played in preparing them for it. Speaking of Virginia's decision to champion independence, Randolph wrote: "The principles of Paine's pamphlet now stalked in triumph under the sanction of the most extensive, richest and most commanding colony in America." Less than a month later, on June 7, Virginian Richard Henry Lee stood up on the floor of the Pennsylvania Statehouse and proposed that the Continental Congress, on behalf of a united people, declare:

> . . . that these united colonies are and of right ought to be free and independent states; that they are absolved from all allegiance to the British crown and that all political connection between them and the sate of Great Britain is and ought to be totally dissolved.

8

"THE DEVIL IS IN THE PEOPLE"

The popular shift that took place in Virginia, allowing it to play such a decisive part in events of 1776, was an intensified example of the transforming effect *Common Sense* had, to one degree or another, on each of the thirteen provinces. In every one of the colonies, whether they started out as predominantly Whig, Tory, or in between, Paine's pamphlet exerted a powerful, radicalizing traction. In the span of a few short months, Virginia had gone from a divided, Tory-leaning straggler to the extreme vanguard of the pro-independence ranks.

In spite of the depredations of Governor Dunmore and the push by Virginia's tobacco planters to open trade with foreign markets, the sudden, dramatic lurch toward independence came as a surprise to many Virginians. Edmund Randolph, for one, observed at the end of the Virginia assembly's session in the fall of 1775: "The Convention closed their labors for supporting the war without expressing in any act a yearning for independence." They had levied troops, set aside the royal government, and begun to act in some ways like an independent nation. And yet, Edmund Randolph wrote, if the convention had even proposed the idea of independence, there would have risen "a universal clamor against it." This was coming from the same assembly and the same colony that would play the leading part in the collective move toward independence just a few months later.

Randolph, who in addition to serving as a Virginia congressman and governor, U.S. Attorney General, and Secretary of State found time to pen a *History of Virginia*, recalled that the impetus for change had come from an unexpected but no less welcome quarter. He wrote that Virginia changed its mind about independence due to the indispensable exertions of "Thomas Paine, an Englishman by birth and possessing an imagination which happily combined political topics." He recalled that *Common Sense* was remarkable for "the ease with which it insinuated itself into the hearts of the people." Randolph proved himself a perceptive observer when he noted that *Common Sense* was distinguished by "a style hitherto unknown on this side of the Atlantic" as well as Paine's unrelenting focus on the "abuses of the British Government." Paine's argument, Randolph recalled, won over both the "learned" and "unlearned" alike and "the public sentiment, which a few weeks before had shuddered at the tremendous obstacles with which independence was environed, over leaped every barrier."

Thomas Jefferson also recalled in his *Notes on the State of Virginia* that, the support for independence came suddenly to Virginia. Before April of 1776, Jefferson wrote, "Independence, and the establishment of a new form of government, were not even yet the objects of the people at large." Jefferson observed that copies of *Common Sense* had, before that time, only gotten into a "few hands," and, as a result, the idea of independence had not yet been "opened to the mass of the people." Sometime on or before April 20, John Penn reported that, while passing through Virginia on his way to Philadelphia from his home in North Carolina, he discovered that "*Common Sense* and Independence . . . was the cry, throughout Virginia." The important point is that for both men the spread of Paine's pamphlet and public support for independence were one and the same.

George Washington also understood that the seed of independence would not take easily in his native soil. From his headquarters in Cambridge, Massachusetts, he wrote: "My countrymen [meaning Virginians], I know from their form of government and steady attachment heretofore to royalty, will come reluctantly into the idea of independency." But he, himself, had abandoned his own desire for reconciliation only after reading *Common Sense*, and he had reason to hope that it was having a similar effect on his countrymen: " . . . by private letters which I have lately received from Virginia, I find *Common Sense* is working a powerful change there in the minds of many men."

From the other side of the fence, Virginia loyalists also observed, if with somewhat less enthusiasm, the impact *Common Sense* was having on the people. English-born Nicholas Cresswell read a copy of Paine's work with horror, calling it "one of the vilest things that was ever published to the world. Full of false representations, lies, calumny, and treason," expressly intended "to subvert all kingly governments and erect an independent republic." Cresswell was determined to resist the gathering momentum toward separation at all costs, but the times were against him. By the end of the month, he bitterly conceded that "Nothing but independence will go down. The devil is in the people."

Among most Americans, however, the reaction was electric and rapturously positive. This was true not just of those already warm to the idea of independence, but also of others who were still puzzling through their opinions on the matter. Little more than a month after the publication of *Common Sense*, a young acquaintance would write to Nathan Hale:

Whether we ought in point of advantage to declare ourselves an independent state and fight as independents or
still continue to resist as subjects is a question which has
of late very much engross'd in these parts the conversation
of every rank more especially since the appearance of a little pamphlet entitled *Common Sense* . . . . Have you seen
it? Upon my word 'tis well done—'tis what would be common sense were not most men so blinded by their prejudices that their sense of things is not what it ought to be—
I confess a perusal of it has much reformed my notions upon
several points & I own myself a staunch independent and
ground my principles on almost innumerable arguments.

The profound and widespread popular impact of *Common Sense*
was pronounced and unprecedented, but it should not be viewed, at
the end of the day, as a complete surprise. Thomas Paine reached the
largest audience ever by a political writer because he aimed at the
largest audience ever. Ideology, class, or education did not limit his
target. He wrote to inspire Whigs but also to convert Tories. He
made sure his pamphlet was affordable to everyone. Most importantly, he wrote to, for, and of the people. As one historian noted:

Paine was not writing for intellectuals. His target was the
minds and hearts of average Americans, already inflamed
by two years of political and economic turmoil. It was a
historic symbiosis between a revolutionary situation and
the greatest pamphleteer of his time.

Paine's style was intentionally accessible for as wide a segment
of society as possible. It was a style and an intention that grew out of
his firm belief that ideas, politics, and government were within the
intellectual reach of everyone. To bridge the gap between the lan-

guage of "the people" and the traditional language of political discourse, Paine created an entirely new language out of whole cloth. Benjamin Rush said of Paine that he "possessed a wonderful talent of writing to the tempers and feelings of the public." But he also noted the ambidextrous nature of that talent, adding that "his compositions, though full of splendid and original imagery, were always adapted to the common capacities."

The voice he perfected in the pages of *Common Sense* was the voice he had first discovered in Lewes and had refined in his brief career at *Pennsylvania Magazine*. His subject matter was by definition a lofty one—human liberty. His challenge was to remove that subject from the heady realms to which it was usually confined and examine it in the language of everyday discourse—to simplify it without depriving it of its power to inspire. "As it is my design to make those that can scarcely read understand," Paine once wrote, "I shall therefore avoid every literary ornament and put it in language as plain as the alphabet." For the most part, Paine remained true to this dictum. And yet *Common Sense* is full of potent images and beautifully crafted lyrical passages that are some of the most eloquent in American political history.

Common Sense is a work of political philosophy written for those who didn't read works of political philosophy. Paine took the methods of philosophical inquiry—analogy, metaphor, and hyperbole—and adapted them to his audience. Instead of conjuring images out of antiquity or contemporary legal scholarship, he borrowed a page from Franklin's *Poor Richard's Almanac* and drew comparisons with things most people were familiar with in their daily life. Paine was not speaking to a nation of philosophers. He was speaking to a nation of farmers. He would therefore use common agricultural language and similes to illustrate and solidify his philosophical points. He knew that when he told his audience that "now is the seed-time" they would understand that he was telling them to act now or they would reap a poor harvest in the future. Likewise, he knew that they would understand that something engraved small on the bark of a "young oak" would loom large as the tree grew to maturity.

Still, if the popular appeal of *Common Sense* had lain only in its style and language, it is unlikely that it would have had the immediate and universal impact it did. Much has been made, in this book and elsewhere, of the importance *Common Sense* played in the political struggle between Great Britain and the American colonies. But Paine makes clear on nearly every page of his pamphlet that he had larger fish to fry. To him *independence* did not merely imply separation from George III and the British Empire. It represented a complete break with the whole of human history—in his view an almost unbroken string of inequality, oppression, ignorance, and tyranny. Paine fully meant it when he called upon Americans not just to cast off British rule but to create an asylum for liberty.

The average colonist, truth be told, did not feel too directly oppressed by the taxes meted out by the English Parliament. Most Americans, in fact, had very little at stake in the debate over internal versus external taxes or over tariffs levied by Parliament versus a more local governmental body. Most of the taxes that had caused all the disputes were invisible to the final consumer having been paid by an importer or a merchant when they were first brought ashore. And if a farmer in western Massachusetts did end up having to pay it, what did it matter to them if it ended up in a coffer in Boston or one in London? The deeper popular appeal of *Common Sense* lay in the fact that it did not present independence as a way to escape a monarchy but as a way to achieve democracy. As Paine would later reflect:

> The mere independence of America, were it to have been followed by a system of government modeled after the corrupt system of English government, would not have interested me with the unabated ardor that it did. It

was to bring forward and establish the representative system of government, as the work itself will show, that was
the leading principle with me in writing.

This republican vision, more than anything else, differentiated
Common Sense from every other utterance on the subject of independence. And this vision sustained the American people through
almost eight years of war and sacrifice—the belief that their cause
was larger than themselves and even larger than their country, that
they were fighting on behalf of their posterity and, indeed, on behalf
of "all mankind."

"No taxation without representation." The slogan, which by
1776 had been circulating for over a decade, is often cited as principle of colonial resistance, but while it was no doubt dear to some, it
is not a very compelling *causi bellum*. The true cause for which the
people of America shouldered the burden of a war against the most
powerful nation on earth is one they heard for the first time in
Common Sense. Thomas Paine challenged Americans with the idea
that, from out of a centuries-long legacy of tyranny, oppression, and
inequality, "We have it in our power to begin the world over again."

For their part, the American people reacted to *Common Sense* as
if they knew it was their own. Its enemies became their enemies;
Plain Truth and other pamphlets against *Common Sense* were publicly
burned, and, in one case, a shop that printed it was attacked by an
angry mob. The king's coat of arms, which hung in the assembly halls
throughout the provinces, were taken down and ceremoniously
burned; his portraits were turned to the wall. And Paine's ideas
became the public's ideas. Letters from readers flooded the pages of
newspapers, endorsing the doctrine of *Common Sense*, praising its
author, and calling for independence. "You have declared the sentiments of millions," wrote one Connecticut Yankee, "Your production
may justly be compared to a land-flood that sweeps all before it."

Another citizen wrote in the *New York Journal* praising " . . . your famous pamphlet *Common Sense*, by which I am convinced of the necessity of independency, to which I was before averse."

The remarkable extent to which *Common Sense* "insinuated itself into the hearts of the people" was further illustrated by the frequency with the language of rebellion came to reflect Paine's. In their petition for instructing their delegates to vote in favor of independence, the citizens of Malden, Massachusetts, repeated phrases from *Common Sense* almost word for word. They expressed their desire "to have no further connection with a King who can unfeelingly hear of the slaughter of his subjects, and composedly sleep with their blood upon his soul."

In addition to independence, Paine's advocacy of an American Republic—founded on the equality of man and governed, however, according to a constitution of their own making—offered the people a concrete objective toward which to aspire. Such a plan of government, however, was not unanimously admired. Many American loyalists opposed independence out of a fundamental belief in the superiority of the monarchical system of government. Other Tories, and even many moderate Whigs, feared independence not out of an attachment to Great Britain or its institutions, but out of a lack of confidence that Americans were prepared to govern themselves. They did not fear independence so much as they feared what would come after independence. Because they could find no example of a modern republic, many doubted the practicability of such government, and they expressed distrust in the ability of a free people to govern themselves. If they were Whigs, this often led them to favor the notion of a "continental monarchy" to replace the British one. On the other hand, loyalists, like the author of *Plain Truth*, warned that the connection to England should be preserved and that " . . . if the doctrines of *Common Sense* were adopted then the entire country would immediately degenerate into democracy." Paine's call for republican government, by contrast, demonstrated a fundamental confidence in the American people—a confidence that began in his personal belief that all men were created equal and that was strengthened by his observations over the time since he had come to America. He would later recall that:

> During the suspension of the old governments in America, both prior to and at the breaking out of hostilities, I was struck with the order and decorum with which everything was conducted.

Where others saw "democracy" as a dangerous unknown, Paine saw it as an attainable ideal. As common as it is today to look back on the Revolution and see independence and democracy as two sides of the same coin, among Paine's contemporaries it was not necessarily so. Before *Common Sense*, the word "republic" was a pejorative term that smacked of utopianism and anarchy. After *Common Sense*, it was the determined objective of a nation.

In 1815 John Adams wrote to Thomas Jefferson that, in his opinion, the Revolution had occurred not in the halls of Congress or on the battlefield, but rather in the "minds of the people." In spite of his deserved eminence among the ranks of revolutionary leaders, Adams recognized that the movement toward independence had come from the bottom up rather than the top down. At the time, Adams, together with his staunchest allies, believed that the momentous step toward independence could and should have been taken in Congress only *after* "the voice of the people drove us to it." When the call came, it came more abruptly and more forcefully than even the most avid *independent* expected. Within a few short weeks, the Continental Congress went from trying to explore ways to turn the public mind toward independence to answering charges from their constituents that they were acting too slowly in declaring independence. To most observers, the primary cause of the sudden change was *Common Sense*, which had, according to Samuel Adams, "awakened the public mind, and led the people loudly to call for a declaration of our national independence."

That the Congress was so nearly outflanked on the march toward independence was largely due to the sudden, direct impact *Common Sense* had on the people of the thirteen colonies. The ideas of *Common Sense* did not filter down to the people from the pundits and politicians above because it was intended by its author to speak directly to the people. In this way, *Common Sense* was revolutionary in the broadest sense of the word. By arguing in favor of republican government, Paine was advocating democracy in theory. But by addressing that argument to the American people directly, he was facilitating democracy in fact.

9

A PEOPLE'S ARMY

On New Year's Day 1776, at the army headquarters in Cambridge, General Washington gave the order for the new "Continental" flag, replete with thirteen stripes, to be flown for the first time. After six months as the army's commander in chief, he had little reason to welcome the turn of the calendar and even less to celebrate the holiday. Poorly equipped and insufficiently armed, Washington's army was hemorrhaging scores and even hundreds of troops a day as their enlistments expired with the old year. The occupying British garrison, enjoying the shelter and comfort of Boston, were well aware of the sorry state of the rebel force opposing them. On the first morning of 1776, from the other side of the Charles River in the dim light of dawn, the British troops watched the new flag inch its way up the flagpole and mistook the unfamiliar colors. They assumed that the ridiculous, amateur American army had at last come to their senses and were raising a flag of surrender.

While British lookouts underestimated their opponent, conditions were indeed desperate, and no one felt it more than Washington. From a high of 15,000 men in June, he was now down to almost half that number. As whole regiments departed *en masse*, he was forced to rotate volunteers and militia to give the appearance to the enemy that his defenses were fully manned. The men were adequately dressed against the New England winter, but the supply of powder was less than thirty rounds per soldier. For all these material privations, however, the scarcity that pained him most was "a dearth of public spirit and want of virtue."

Insubordination and lack of attention to duty were too prevalent, felt Washington, and his greatest concern was the unwillingness of his experienced troops to re-enlist after their terms had expired. This left him with the almost impossible task of essentially disbanding one army and recruiting another and doing it "within musket shot of two and twenty regiments, the flowers of the British army." His officers tried to cajole their men into re-enlisting by an escalating scale of coercion—appealing first to their patriotism, then promising furlough, next bullying with extra work detail, and finally threatening to throw them in the brig for their remaining days. Washington decried the lack of resolve and purpose that he saw pervading his ranks—especially the New Englanders whose homes were enticingly near. "The Connecticut troops will not be prevailed upon to stay longer than their term," he wrote in early January, "and such a dirty, mercenary spirit pervades the whole, that I should not be surprised at any disaster that may happen."

This lack of commitment appeared to be a result of the fact that the rank and file did not have a clear overriding cause to rally behind in the first year of the war—certainly not one commensurate to the sacrifice they were being asked to make. Before independence, these soldiers were being asked to leave their homes and families to suffer privation and risk their lives in defense of a country that did not exist against an enemy with which they hoped to reconcile. Many of them had entered the Continental army by swearing allegiance to the same king their British adversaries swore allegiance to. What, then, was their ultimate purpose? To re-establish their rights under a constitution they did not know? To contest a distant Parliament's right to levy taxes, which few of them would ever have to pay? Their red-coated enemies knew what their own purpose was—to put down these upstart rebels and preserve the British Empire. So what were these Americans—armed provincials but recently called from their plows and fishing nets—fighting for?

To answer his shortage of equipment, powder, and recruits, Washington wrote frequent, occasionally sharp letters to the Continental Congress. To address the deficiency of morale among his troops, the commander in chief was at a loss. Then, toward the end of January, Washington came across a new pamphlet from Philadelphia addressed "to the inhabitants of America" and advocating immediate independence from Great Britain. He was told that it was having an unprecedented influence wherever it was read. So moved was Washington by the argument of *Common Sense* that he ordered copies of the pamphlet distributed among all the ranks of his army and saw to it that it was read aloud to any who could not read it for themselves.

While it was instantly popular throughout the Continental army, *Common Sense* was, for several reasons, greeted with particular enthusiasm by many of Washington's officers. After eight months of war, many officers had first-hand knowledge of the disadvantages the country faced in going up against the well-trained, well-equipped professional troops of the British Empire. They understood before others that, if the colonies were to win the "war," they would have to have military and financial help from abroad. Some prescient officers, such as Nathanial Greene, had privately determined, and publicly opined, that such aid would only come when and if the war became a war for independence. More than a week before *Common Sense* was published, Greene had written that a declaration of independence would "call upon the world, and the great God who governs it, to witness the necessity, propriety and rectitude thereof."

Brigadier General John Sullivan was another one of the Officer Corps who was an early and eager proponent of independence. He was wintered down at the army's encampment in Cambridge when he read Paine's words, and they only fueled his impatience for a separation. To his friend John Adams in Philadelphia he wrote "I have seen *Common Sense* and admire it." Then he scrawled in the margin, "*and wish that your Brethren had a Sufficient share of it*" before concluding, "I hope so Rational a Doctrine will be Established throughout the Continent."

But most officers, including Washington, had not yet concluded that independence was necessarily desirable or possible by the time they read *Common Sense*. General Charles Lee wrote to his Commander on January 24: "Have you seen the pamphlet *Common Sense?* I never saw such a masterly, irresistible performance. . . . In short, I own myself convinced, by the arguments, of the necessity of separation." Edmund Randolph, then Washington's aide-de-camp at Cambridge, noted that many pro-independence officers used *Common Sense* as a "text book" with which to instruct their sluggish, indecisive comrades.

On a more personal level, Continental officers also perceived that they stood to gain little for their efforts on behalf of American liberties if, in the end, America became reconciled to Great Britain. It is unlikely that their exertions in service of the rebel army, even in the warmest of rapprochements, would have been rewarded or even recognized within the regular British army. If the war in which they were presently engaged were to culminate in the establishment of an independent republic, however, their prospects would be far brighter. Certainly many of those who had led the war effort could look forward to futures in the new nation's army, as well as its government.

Paine volunteered for the army in the summer of 1776, serving as an aide-de-camp to his friend General Nathanial Greene. Throughout the war, according to Benjamin Rush, the author of

Common Sense was warmly received among officers who always had a place of honor for him at their tables. Needless to say, this admiration for Paine did not extend to English officers. Upon one occasion, advancing British forces took possession of a hastily evacuated American officers' barracks noting, "They have left some poor pork, a few greasy proclamations and some of that scoundrel Common Sense man's letters."

As with the population at large, *Common Sense* found a particularly fond audience among the army's common working people. As Washington no doubt realized when he gave orders for the pamphlet to be distributed to his troops, *Common Sense* offered him and his army two things they most desperately needed. By calling for them to oppose not "tyranny" but the "tyrant," Paine gave them an actual enemy. By stating with fanatic certainty that the only acceptable outcome of the war was independence, he gave them a cause. A recruitment poster from 1776 told would-be soldiers what they were fighting for with a clarity that would have been impossible in 1775: "For The Defense of the Liberties and Independence of the United States, against the hostile designs of foreign enemies." While we may describe it anecdotally, however, there is ultimately no way to quantify the effect *Common Sense* had on the morale of the Continental army rank and file, beyond observing their officer's approval that "It Takes well with Army."

In addition to giving recruits and veteran soldiers a banner to rally around, the doctrine of *Common Sense* also gave heightened purpose to the sacrifice of those who fought and died. On July 21, 1776, the father of Lieutenant John Patten of Bedford, New Hampshire, recorded his feelings upon hearing of his son's death. The words he wrote in his diary reveal a belief that his son died for a just and worthy cause. In words reminiscent of Paine's own, Patten also lay the blame for his loss on a clearly defined enemy: "[He died] on the 20th day of june . . . defending the just Rights of

America, . . . in the prime of life by means of that wicked Tyranical Brute of Great Britain."

Another soldier, Jeremiah Greenman of Rhode Island, was just eighteen years old when he enlisted in the American army in 1775. By the time the war was over, he had fought on battlefields from Quebec to Philadelphia, been captured twice, and had risen from a private to become Adjutant of his regiment. At the end of the war in 1783, before he began the long walk back to Rhode Island, Greenman hosted a celebratory dinner for his fellow officers. After eight long years of war, they gathered to honor each other and the cause for which they had endured so much hardship and sacrifice. As Greenman recorded in his diary; they raised their glasses together and toasted "the Congress of the year 1776 and Common Sense."

10
THE OTHER
FOUNDING FATHERS

JOHN ADAMS

Prior to the publication of *Common Sense*, perhaps no man in America had a better understanding of the challenges and obstacles that stood in the way of American independence than John Adams. That is probably because no other politician had given it more sustained, concentrated consideration. Adams knew that, while he and his allies might push for independence on the floor of the Pennsylvania Statehouse, the ultimate step toward independence could only come once the people were convinced of it—both in terms of the public consciousness and the instructions they gave to their delegates. Adams, himself, had made more than one attempt to persuade the public at large, but his efforts in this direction had been mostly innocuous. His series of letters written as "Novanglus," for instance, are marked by a hesitant, deferent tone and lack the fiery resolve of his utterances in Congress or even of his private correspondence. Even though they were written in 1775, Adams came across sounding more like John Dickinson than himself, and he steered well clear of advocating independence.

Adams was right about the absolute necessity of the issue being decided in the minds of the people before it was decided on the floor of the Congress. What he did not know was how that widespread, popular consensus would be accomplished. After the ineffectual "Novanglus" series, he kept his own attentions focused where they would do the most good—in keeping up the pressure on his colleagues in Congress. In early 1776 he expressed his belief that a difficult task such as winning the people over to the idea of independence would have to be entrusted to the "Design of Providence." By the time he returned to Philadelphia in February, exactly a month after *Common Sense* went on sale, it must have seemed to him that such a "design" was indeed at work in the city. "Scarcely a Paper comes out," Adams marveled just a few days after his return, "without a Speculation or two in open Vindication of opinions, which Five Months ago were Said to be unpopular." Only two months later, he would observe with satisfaction "that all are now united in the great Question"—the question of independence. Most of the witnesses to this profound, abrupt change in the popular mind, in Philadelphia and throughout the colonies, saw it as a result almost entirely of *Common Sense*.

Adams also believed that the southern provinces would ultimately determine which way the balance between independence and reconciliation would tip. Before 1776 the southern colonies had always added their weight to the Tory side. As the observations of Washington, Jefferson, Edmund Randolph, and others made plain, it was *Common Sense* that coursed through Virginia and the other southern states, inspiring them to lead the call for independence.

Another of Adams' nagging worries was that, even if public sentiments had started to swing toward independence, any unexpected concessions on the part of the British could have thrown the entire situation into a confusion of second guessing and renewed division between American Tories and Whigs. As Adams wrote to

Abigail in the weeks when *Common Sense* was becoming the "common faith," prospects for a vote in favor of independence appeared promising "unless the cunning Ministry, by proposing Negociations and Terms of Reconciliation, should divert the present Current from its Channell." Adams' fear in this regard underestimated both British intransigence and the thoroughness with which *Common Sense* would turn the mind of the American public against the British government, its leaders, and its institutions, making negotiation unlikely and capitulation impossible.

Finally, Adams was vexed by the question of the right time to push the question of independence to a head. He once compared the challenge of getting all thirteen colonies to call for independence with one voice to the difficulty of synchronizing thirteen clocks to strike the hour at the same moment. Just as Adams feared the consequences of Congress running out ahead of the rest of the country and proposing independence before the people were ready, he was also haunted by the danger that they would act too late. Adams fully understood that the British position became stronger with each passing week. If America waited too long to declare their independence, the British would have so thoroughly garrisoned the colonies as to make armed support of that declaration impossible. Paine's pamphlet not only appeared at precisely the right moment but also moved with such astonishing speed through each of thirteen colonies that the change that Adams envisioned as occurring in the span of months and years occurred instead within a span of days and weeks. As a result, Boston remained the solitary stronghold of the British in America. By the time the Declaration of Independence was signed, they had lost even that.

Recognizing the effect of *Common Sense* in overcoming these barriers, Adams was at first inclined to give credit where it was due, finding some to criticize but much to praise in Paine's work. As time went by, however, he grew gradually more dismissive of Paine and the importance of *Common Sense*. Adams had labored long and sacrificed much in the service of the founding of his country—of that there can be no doubt. To that service, he brought a remarkable array of talents, in addition to integrity and vision. But another aspect of Adams personality—one that has been remarked upon by his admirers and detractors during his lifetime and up until today— was a pronounced sense of vanity and an outsized fixation on his reputation in history. (Incidentally, these are the two qualities that Paine was also most frequently accused of possessing.) While this quality rarely affected his behavior or judgment during critical events, it often colored his subsequent reflections upon those events and the other figures involved in them. "John Adams was a great congressional politician" says Revolutionary historian Thomas Flemming, "and justly famed as the architect of the decision for independence, but he was not a reliable reporter." Adams was a perceptive observer whose diaries and letters are marked by a gift for detail and a clear, expressive writing style. His flaws as a reporter of events and people derive not from carelessness or obtuseness but from a perhaps unconscious agenda concerning his share of the glory in the success of the Revolution.

It would have come as a surprise to many that Adams, the man who had so publicly nominated Washington to be commander in chief, would privately complain, as he watched the General ride off to assume command of the army outside Boston:

> Such is the pride and pomp of war. I, poor creature,
> worn out with scribbling for bread and my liberty, low
> in spirits and weak in health, must leave other to wear
> the laurels which I have sown.

When he read in an English newspaper that Franklin was being called the "Founder of the American Empire," Adams predicted, only half in jest, that there was a campaign of propaganda underfoot to name the eighteenth century the "Franklinian Age" or *"le Siècle Franklinnien."* In a similar spirit, he would later make the back-handed prediction that the period would instead be called the "Age of Paine." One gets the sense while reading Adams' reflections upon the other great figures of his time that what was really bothering him was the fact that no one was proposing "the age of Adams" or the *"le Siècle Adamsienne."* Dr. Franklin, at the height of their personal difficulties, nonetheless, gave a fair, insightful appraisal of Adams "I am persuaded . . . that he means well for his Country, is always an honest Man, often a Wise One, but sometimes and in some things, absolutely out of his Senses."

As time went on, Adams grew more and more dismissive of Paine and of the pamphlet that was so pivotal in the success of his own endeavors on behalf of independence. Shortly after *Common Sense* was published, Adams had noted with approval the effect it was having and pronounced that it contained "a great deal of good sense, delivered in a clear, simple, concise and nervous Style." After the war, Adams conceded that "It has been a general Opinion that this pamphlet was of great Importance in the Revolution," but was non-committal as to whether he shared that opinion. Finally—writing many years later and after Paine's death—he derided *Common Sense* simply as a "poor, short-sighted crapulous mass." As Eric Foner has written, "John Adams always resented the fact that *Common Sense* was credited with having contributed so much to the movement for independence." That Adams' resentment prevented him from turning his considerable powers of observation objectively on Thomas Paine and *Common Sense* is unfortunate. Few would have been better positioned to give a detailed account of the many ways in which the revolutionary landscape shifted during the pamphlet's unprecedented run. As a prolific and much quoted chronicler of the period, Adams' words could have done much to secure for Paine the share of recognition almost all of his contemporaries felt he had earned.

BENJAMIN FRANKLIN

When Benjamin Franklin first encouraged Thomas Paine to emigrate from England to America, he had no inkling whatsoever that his protégé would have so profound an effect on the nervous status quo then existing between the two countries. Although vouching for Paine as a "worthy, ingenious young man," Franklin asked his son-in-law to help find him work merely as a "clerk . . . assistant tutor . . . or assistant surveyor." He would have been almost as surprised to learn that he himself would be leaving England, in bitterness, less than six months after Paine.

Franklin had spent most of the previous eighteen years in London and had been a staunch defender of American rights, as well as an eloquent advocate of the mutual benefits of a continued connection. By the time he boarded the Pennsylvania packet in Portsmouth in March of 1775, however, he had lost much of his admiration for England and become convinced of the pettiness, corruption, and venality of British leaders. He had also come to the realization that the current government, in its arrogance, would never propose or accept a compromise with its American subjects and that the dispute would eventually be settled by blows.

Franklin's thinking upon the American question, like Paine's, had been influenced by the anti-government ideas of London's radical Whigs and the Commonwealth men. Like Paine, once he adopted the cause of American independence, he became one of its most passionate and determined supporters. He was heartened, upon returning home, to find his fellow Philadelphians arming for war in the weeks after Lexington and Concord, even if they were uncertain of what the war would achieve. When he asked Thomas Paine in the

Fall of 1775, to write a pamphlet on the Anglo-American conflict, he no doubt intended the piece to sharpen his countrymen's ideas of what it was they were fighting for and against.

In subsequent years, Franklin frequently acknowledged the importance of *Common Sense* and its "great effect on the mind of the people." He and Paine remained friends and correspondents until Franklin's death in 1790, exchanging views upon American affairs as well their mutual interests in other, scientific subjects ranging from smokeless candles to Paine's design for an iron bridge to span Philadelphia's Schuylkill River. In the few years between Franklin's return from France in 1785 and Paine's own departure for Europe in 1787, the younger man was a frequent dinner guest at the great doctor's house, where the two would occasionally while away an entire evening conducting practical experiments of one sort or another. Paine's regard for Franklin never diminished, and he always spoke of him in terms bordering on reverence. For his part, Franklin always remained proud of the fact that he had been instrumental in Paine's career, encouraging him to come to America: "Be assured, my dear friend, that . . . I value my self on the Share I had in procuring for [America] the acquisition of so useful and valuable a Citizen."

GEORGE WASHINGTON

In the summer of 1775, the New York assembly passed a resolution of support for the newly appointed commander in chief, then marching north to assume command of the Continental army. In doing so, they showed a glimpse of how they saw the present struggle with Britain ending. They expressed their hope for the speedy resolution of the war and shared "the fondest wish of every American soul, an accommodation with our mother country." In accepting the appointment, Washington harbored similar hopes for the future. He wrote to his family that, while gratified by the honor, he fully expected the war to be over by the fall and for the colonies to still be a part of the British Empire.

When Washington wrote of Virginians' predisposition to royalty and their native reluctance to independence, he was also speaking, at least in part, of his own beliefs. He saw no irony in the fact that he could lead troops against the British garrison in Boston at the same time as he lead his officers in toasting the king's health. When Washington wrote that "I find *Common Sense* is working a powerful change there in the minds of many men," he was again betraying some of his own feelings. He first read the pamphlet toward the end of January. Washington biographer, James Thomas Flexner writes:

> Washington, who had, up to this time, sought compromise rather than an independent empire, began to change his mind. He was deeply impressed by Thomas Paine's arguments and exhortations in *Common Sense*. On January 31, 1776, Washington first acknowledged in writing the possibility of independence. Four days later, he urged Congress to notify Great Britain that "if nothing else could satisfy a tyrant and his diabolical ministry, we are determined to shake off all connections with a state so unjust and unnatural."

Even if he had not expressed them in writing, Washington had almost certainly entertained thoughts of separation before he read *Common Sense*. It was what he called the "sound doctrine and unanswerable reasoning" of Paine's pamphlet that solidified his belief in the righteousness and the practicability of independence.

Indeed the 'sound doctrine' of *Common Sense* not only changed the minds of his soldiers and officers, it also fundamentally changed the scope. The General recognized that what had begun as a limited conflict of colonial resistance was now a war with universal implications and, in words that echoed Paine's, he addressed his troops accordingly—telling them that "the fate of unborn Millions" depended on their success.

The change in the ultimate objective of the war also entailed a change in the strategy by which it would be conducted. Early on, Washington had pursued an approach of trying to force the British into a single large-scale battle or campaign that would decide the war by demonstrating American resolve and forcing the British to compromise. A war for independence, Washington understood, meant just the opposite: a drawn-out, grueling contest of attrition that would end not in negotiation but in surrender. Accordingly, the strategy Washington adopted in 1776, and held to for the rest of the war, was one of keeping up the pressure on his enemy, while avoiding an all-out battle that might destroy his army in a single blow.

After the war, Washington was active in seeing that Paine was rewarded by Congress for his service during the Revolution, not just for *Common Sense* but also for his other works written in service of the American cause and for which the author had consistently refused payment. His task was not made any easier by the fact that the prickly, temperamental Paine had won almost as many enemies among the delegates as he had admirers. Washington's influence proved decisive, however, and Paine was ultimately awarded a modest emolument.

THOMAS JEFFERSON

In January of 1776, Thomas Jefferson, like John Adams, was not in Philadelphia but at home in Virginia. On February 1, another Virginia delegate, Thomas Nelson, closed a letter he had written to Jefferson by adding "P.S. I send you a present of 2/ worth of *Common Sense*." What Jefferson first thought upon reading the pamphlet he did not record. His ultimate opinion, though, was that the sudden shift of Virginians away from Britain and toward independence was the direct result of *Common Sense*. He observed that his countrymen, by early 1776, had not yet called for independence and republican government because Paine's pamphlet had not yet reached the general public.

Once he arrived in Philadelphia, on May 14, Jefferson marveled at the change that had taken place in the city and more importantly in the Pennsylvania Statehouse. In *Common Sense*, Paine suggested that the Continental Congress formulate a "manifesto" describing the many "miseries" Americans had endured at the hands of their British masters, as well as "the peaceable methods we have ineffectually used for redress." Such a document should also, he continued, declare that "not being able, any longer, to live happily or safely under the cruel disposition of the British court, we have been driven to the necessity of breaking off all connection with her." On June 11, the Congress created a committee to draft a Declaration of Independence, and it fell to Thomas Jefferson to bring it into execution.

Jefferson's Declaration marked a formal departure, on the part of the Continental Congress, from all previous actions and proclamations they had undertaken. The most obvious divergence was the adoption of separation from Great Britain as the official objective of the united colonies. To justify this action, Jefferson put forth a radical new view of the nature of government and of the Anglo-American conflict. It was the view that the American people had adopted only recently and one that they had first encountered in the pages of *Common Sense*.

First and foremost, Jefferson's preamble made clear that the ensuing declaration was in no way grounded upon the points of law contained in the British constitution or even the royal charters by which the colonies were brought into existence. Instead Jefferson appealed, just as Paine did, to the timeless, universal authority of the "laws of

Nature and of Nature's God." In doing so he, too, superseded virtually every legal argument that had been made against independence.

After an eloquent elaboration on the primacy of natural law, Jefferson launched into a barrage of repetitive accusations, not against the Parliament or the ministry but against the king himself. Continuing the attack that Paine had begun in *Common Sense*, Jefferson placed the responsibility and the blame solely on the English monarch:

> He has refused his assent to laws the most wholesome and necessary for the public good . . . .
> He has obstructed the administration of justice . . . .
> He has kept among us, in time of peace, standing armies . . . .
> He has plundered our seas, ravaged our coasts, burnt our towns, & destroyed the lives of our people.

By the time he was through, the pleasant fiction of "ministerial" culpability had been banished once and for all from the colonist's vocabulary. Just as sure as their objective was now independence, their enemy had become George III.

The ideas of *Common Sense* echo throughout Jefferson's Declaration, not merely in defense of independence but also in support of a new system of government. Without predicting the imminent establishment of an American Republic as Paine did, Jefferson nonetheless conveyed the promise of a new era in human liberty. He asserted not only America's right to self-rule but also the universal principle that if "any form of government" failed to protect the natural rights of its people, it was the people's right, not just to overthrow that particular government but also to create in its place an entirely new kind of government, "laying its foundation on such principles and organizing its powers in such form as to them shall seem most likely to effect their safety and happiness." The true genius of Jefferson's document equals that of Paine's pamphlet. They both represented not merely a defiant break with the past but also an audacious and hopeful vision of the future.

While Jefferson and Paine first became acquainted in Philadelphia, it was not until after the war, when both were in Paris, that they became friends. They shared similar opinions on questions of politics, and religion, as well as a common hope for the French Revolution, which they witnessed the birth of together. The Marquis de Lafayette once recalled the three of them sitting together in Paris for hours in animated discussion upon the fine points of the Constitution, then under debate back in America.

Jefferson and Paine's mutual interest in science also formed a bond that would keep them in correspondence throughout their lives. More than a decade after Paine's death, Jefferson, the author of the most powerful document in American history, said of Paine: "No writer has exceeded Paine in the ease and familiarity of style, in perspicuity of expression, happiness of elucidation, and in simple and unassuming language."

EPILOGUE:

AFTER COMMON SENSE

The creation and signing of the Declaration of Independence represented a culmination of the energies generated and intensified by *Common Sense*. With the coming of the larger war that he had done so much to bring about, Paine turned his efforts and now formidable influence to the support and ultimate success of that war. From the summer of 1776 until the Treaty of Paris, which ended the war in 1783, Paine's pen was ceaselessly active in the service of America's cause. Signing many of his later works simply "by *Common Sense*," Paine nurtured a persona that commanded the attention of the nation throughout the Revolution, rallying his compatriots against despair, cautioning them of unseen dangers, and restraining them from overconfidence. As he did with *Common Sense*, Paine directed the profits of his other popular wartime writings to the support of the war effort.

Less than a month after July 4, 1776, Paine joined the Continental army as an aide-de-camp to General Nathanial Greene. Shouldering a musket and sharing the hardships of Washington's men, Paine marched with them during the dismal New York campaign and the retreat across New Jersey. He spent his evenings in General Greene's tent, hunched over a drumhead he used as a writing table to scribble dispatches for publication in the Philadelphia newspapers. In December of 1776, during one of the darkest periods of the war, Paine undertook what would become his second greatest contribution to the Revolution when he began a brilliant series of pamphlets called the *American Crisis*.

The end of the war and the achievement of American independence did not mark an end to Paine's exertions on behalf of the newborn republic. In *Common Sense*, he had called for the formation of a convention to oversee the creation of an American Magna Carta that would set forth the rights of the American people, as well as the powers and limitations of their government. The Constitutional Convention first met on May 25, 1787, with the intention of creating just such a document. Paine wrote passionately and eloquently in support of the Convention's efforts and of a strong central government to unite the recently liberated colonies. After little more than a year of debate and compromise, the Convention ratified the United States Constitution on June 21, 1788, and the United States of America took its present form.

With the foundation of the American Republic well begun, Paine's thoughts returned to the old world and to the idea, first expressed in *Common Sense*, that the principles of the American Revolution might, with help, spread to the entrenched monarchies of Europe. "Where liberty is not, there is my home," Paine once told Benjamin Franklin. He left for Europe in April of 1787. Although already somewhat famous throughout the continent as the author of *Common Sense*, he would soon rise to a prominence almost as great as he enjoyed in America during the war.

He wrote two great pamphlets while in Europe: *Rights of Man*, written in defense of the early French Revolution, and *The Age of Reason*, a devastating attack on accepted religious traditions and the ways in which those traditions were used to solidify the power of corrupt, illegitimate, monarchical governments. As had his first great pamphlet, these much larger works summarized many of the ideas that had been confined within an intellectual elite and introduced them to a much wider popular audience. They became, in turn, the two best-selling works of eighteenth century Europe. In spite of their immense popularity, the time had not yet arrived in Europe for the type of sweeping changes Paine recommended. If his later writings did not have the same immediate and dramatic effect upon European events that *Common Sense* had had in America, his voice had lost none of its influence to provoke the powerful.

In 1792, Paine was forced to flee England because of the unprecedented popularity of the recently published *Rights of Man*. He departed from Dover only minutes ahead of the officers sent to arrest him for sedition. In revolutionary France, Paine used his position as an honorary member of the National Convention to support the principles of liberty and equality and occasionally to criticize the revolution itself when he felt its leaders acted contrary to those principles. As the tide of the revolution drifted toward chaos, Paine time and again raised his voice to remind them that a constitution was needed to avoid the abuse of power by governments, even democratic ones. He courageously condemned the excesses of the reign of terror—the "avidity to punish" as well as the arbitrary, self-serving use of power. Speaking through a translator, he stood alone on the floor of the convention to oppose the execution of the doomed Louis XVI. Paine knew that he was speaking in a "day of danger" and that men were beheaded every day in the *Place de la Revolution* for far less provocation than he was offering.

On December 28, 1793, at the height of the terror, Paine was arrested and held in the Luxembourg Prison—a place of brief confinement for thousands who would meet their end at the sharp edge of Dr. Guillotine's invention. Luckily, he would escape that fate, but only just. It remains one of the remarkable ironies of Paine's life—and a testament to the strength of his convictions—that he would narrowly evade arrest for his condemnation of one "crowned ruffian" only to be imprisoned and nearly executed for his defense of another. For thirteen months Paine languished in the shadow of the guillotine until, after the downfall of Robespierre, the new American Minister to France, James Monroe, was able to secure his release.

Paine returned to America in 1802 to discover that his more recently published works had surrounded his name with controversy. Having consigned their revolutionary legacy to the history books, most Americans were content with a more gradual pace of social and political change. While the works he had written in Europe had sold well in America, his political and especially his religious views were not in line with general *zeitgeist* in the same way that his writings during the war had been. His ideas would continue to have influence and find champions among American as diverse as Walt Whitman, Abraham Lincoln, and Thomas Edison. At the dawn of the new century however, his views on women's rights, slavery, and political and economic equality were ahead of their time. When he died in New York City, in 1809, at the age of seventy-two, the news provoked only a fraction of the outpouring it would have, had he met his end a generation earlier. Countless statues and memorials would have sprung up in all the colonies of the young republic, speeches would have been given, and reminiscences published. Paine's reputation as the author of *Common Sense* had been eclipsed by his international reputation for his more controversial later works.

But it was the revolutionary hero, Thomas Paine, *Common Sense* himself, for whom George Washington, in 1784, interceded in Congress. Washington recommended that a gift of some sort be made to Paine for the services rendered to the American cause. Paine would eventually reap considerable financial rewards for his later writings, but he had refused to profit from those he penned during the war. As a result, he teetered on the brink of poverty. No one knew better than Washington the crucial role Paine and his pen had played during the darkest, most uncertain, hours of his country's history.

In the Winter of 1776, the outlook for the Continental army was as grim as it would be at any time in the war. The flush of hope and confidence that had accompanied the Declaration of Independence had since been replaced by the sense of unrelenting failure on battlefields throughout New York and New Jersey, where the only "victories" came in the form of well-executed retreats. To end the year on such a grim note would have a demoralizing effect not just on the American troops in the field, but on the people as a whole. Working in Washington's camp, Paine had sensed the mood of his compatriots and wrote the *American Crisis* to reassure and re-inspire them with some of the spirit of the preceding summer. His words were as much a challenge to the American people as they were a tribute to the soldiers with whom he marched:

> These are the times that try men's souls. The summer sol-dier and the sunshine patriot will, in this crisis, shrink from the service of their country; but he that stands it now deserves the love and thanks of man and woman. Tyranny, like hell, is not easily conquered; yet we have this consolation with us, that the harder the conflict, the more glorious the triumph. What we obtain too cheap, we esteem too lightly: it is dearness only that gives every thing its value.

Omitting his given name, which was still not well known in the country, Paine instead signed his work with the now famous sobri-quet "Common Sense." At 2 A.M. on December 26, upon the banks the Delaware River, Washington ordered that copies of Paine's new pamphlet be distributed throughout the ranks and that these words be read to his men as they were packed into the flat-bottomed

Durham Boats that would take them across the river to the battle of Trenton. Marching all night, Washington's cold and fatigued troops attacked the town and its unsuspecting garrison of Hessian mercenaries at 8 o'clock in the morning. The sounds of the first shots were mingled with the cries of the Americans shouting lines from the *American Crisis* as they ran through the sleeping streets. By 9:30 the British garrison had surrendered. Washington and his men had their victory, to which they would add the taking of Princeton a week later. More importantly, the American people would begin the New Year with a new spark of hope in their cause. They read accounts of the Battles of Trenton and Princeton just as the *American Crisis* was being distributed throughout the colonies—hardening their determination and sharpening their sense of what they were fighting for. Once again, exactly a year after the publication of *Common Sense*, Paine's writing seized the consciousness of the people and played an important role in the critical events of the day.

It was this aspect of Paine's career that Washington felt deserved the thanks of an indebted country. He understood how Paine had articulated the cause of America and how he had defended and supported that cause in its least auspicious hours, not only in January of 1776, but also throughout the war. Washington's words on Paine's behalf are as appropriate today as they were when they were written in 1784. He asked: "Must the merits, and Services of *Common Sense* continue to glide down the stream of time, unrewarded by this Country?"

For all his international success and involvement in the affairs of other nations, Paine, too, desired and expected that he should be remembered first and foremost as the author of *Common Sense*. He fully realized that it had been his finest hour—as a writer, as a patriot, and as a champion of liberty. It was the greatest cause of his epoch and the one for which he had risked and contributed the most. As Paine later reflected:

I saw, or at least thought I saw, a vast scene opening itself to the world in the affairs of America; and it appeared to me that unless the Americans changed the plan they were then pursuing with respect to the government of England, and declare themselves independent, they would not only involve themselves in a multiplicity of new difficulties, but shut out the prospect that was then offering itself to mankind through their means. It was from these motives that I published *Common Sense*, which is the first work I ever did publish: and so far as I can judge of myself, I believe I never should have been known in the world as an author on any subject whatever, had it not been for the affairs of America.

APPENDIX

COMMON SENSE

NOTES ON THE
FIRST BRADFORD EDITION

The text reproduced in the following pages is the "enlarged version" printed on February 14, 1776, by printers William and Thomas Bradford.

The unexpected and extraordinary success of their joint venture did little to cement the working relationship between Robert Bell as publisher and Thomas Paine as author. Although they had had smaller disagreements before *Common Sense* was published—such as Paine's insistence that Bell's two-shilling asking price was too high—their final falling out occurred some weeks later. As we have seen, Paine intended that all the royalties due to him be donated to the hard-pressed, under-equipped Continental forces then suffering through a miserable winter outside Quebec—this in spite of the fact that Paine had advanced the publisher £20 out of his own pocket to defray the costs of printing. Bell and Paine agreed to divide any potential profits in half.

Paine authorized a friend of his, Captain Thomas Pryor, with whom he had collaborated on some articles for the *Pennsylvania Magazine*, to collect the proceeds and oversee the purchase and shipment of the equipment. To the surprise of the author, Pryor called on Bell's shop and was told that their successful collaboration had netted no profits and that there was, consequently, nothing to divide. Paine's own estimate of the profits due him was at least £30, and he threatened to find a new publisher if the matter was not settled fairly. Furthermore, he warned Bell that he was making substantial additions to the original work, which would make the new edition more attractive. When an unmoved Bell announced (and advertised) his intention to publish a second edition of the original pamphlet with or without the author's blessing, the break between the two was complete.

Paine chose the established Philadelphia publishers William and Thomas Bradford to bring out his expanded edition, and, to answer demand, they agreed to contract two more print shops to produce an additional 6,000 copies and get them on the streets as soon as possible. A German translation of the Bradford edition was also commissioned so that *Common Sense* would reach the large portion of Pennsylvanians who spoke and read German. Thus began a race, as well as an advertising war, played out in the Philadelphia press, between Bell on the one hand and the Bradfords on the other—each claiming to be presenting the most authoritative and current version of Paine's pamphlet. An advertisement placed in the *Pennsylvania Evening Post* on Thursday, January 25, is representative of the melee:

> In the press, and will be published as soon as possible, and sold by W. and T. Bradford at the London Coffee-house, Philadelphia, a new edition of COMMON SENSE, addressed to the inhabitants of America, with large and interesting additions by the author, as will be expressed at the time of publication, among which will be a seasonable and friendly admonition to the people called QUAKERS.

The advertisement then addresses Bell and his unauthorized edition in words probably written by Paine himself:

TO THE PUBLIC

The encouragement and reception which this pamphlet hath already met with, and the great demand for the same, hath induced the publisher of the first edition to print a new edition unknown to the author, who expressly directed him not to proceed therein without orders, because that large additions would be made thereto; wherefore the new edition, lately advertised by the printer of the first, is without the intended additions.

That which is now in the press, and which, by appointment of the author, will be sold as above, and at other such places as will be mentioned at the time of advertising, will, notwithstanding the additions, be reduced to one half of the price of the former edition, with allowance to those who take quantities, in order to accommodate it to the abilities of every man.

Several hundreds are already bespoke, one thousand for Virginia.

Ultimately, the Bradford Enlarged Edition reproduced here was published on February 14, 1776. In addition to the time necessary to write the "new materials," the delay leading up to the publication gave Paine the opportunity of incorporating a reply to "any Attempt to refute the Doctrine of Independence." Apparently—at least in Paine's opinion—no worthy refutation had appeared in the press, as no space is given to answering them in the Enlarged Edition. The additions that Paine does make are a small introduction, an appendix, and the address to the Quakers, all included here. The appendix briefly trumpets the happy coincidence that saw Common Sense and the king's speech opening the new session of parliament appearing in Philadelphia on the exact same day. Paine uses this bit of serendipity as an excuse to launch a fresh assault on the king's character, asserting that the speech justified and validated the language and substance of the condemnation that shocked so many readers of the first edition.

Paine's address to the "People called Quakers" is remarkable for several reasons. In addition to challenging the logic of a recently published piece affirming the loyalty of the Quakers to George III, Paine takes the authors of the piece to task for presuming to speak for the entire Quaker community. (One must remember that, while he was not an active member, Paine had been raised in the Quaker tradition and that it was still the denomination to which he felt most closely attached.) Paine closes the address by picking up a theme that remains a hotly contested one even in our own time, voicing his hope that "the example which you have so unwisely set, of mingling religion with politics, *may be disavowed and reprobated by every in habitant of America.*"

Common Sense went through 56 editions in its first year of publication and continues to be in print to this day. The Bradford Enlarged Edition, also sometimes referred to as the "second edition," has come to be regarded as the closest thing to a standard edition that exists for this endlessly reprinted work.

COMMON SENSE;

ADDRESSED TO THE

INHABITANTS

OF

AMERICA,

On the following interesting

SUBJECTS:

I.   Of the Origin and Design of Government in general, with concise Remarks on the English Constitution.

II. Of Monarchy and Hereditary Succession.

III. Thoughts on the present State of American Affairs.

IV. Of the present ability of America, with some miscellaneous Reflections.

A NEW EDITION, with several Additions in the Body of the work.   To which is Added an APPENDIX ; together with an Address to the People called QUAKERS.

Man knows no Master save creating HEAVEN,
Or those whom choice and common Good ordain.
THOMSON.

PHILADELPHIA:
PRINTED and SOLD by W. and T. BRADFORD

M,DCC,LXXVI.

[PRICE ONE BRITISH SHILLING.]

INTRODUCTION

PERHAPS the sentiments contained in the following pages, are not yet sufficiently fashionable to procure them general favor; a long habit of not thinking a thing *wrong*, gives it a superficial appearance of being *right*, and raises at first a formidable outcry in defence of custom. But the tumult soon subsides. Time makes more converts than reason.

As a long and violent abuse of power, is generally the Means of calling the right of it in question (and in matters too which might never have been thought of, had not the Sufferers been aggravated into the inquiry) and as the Ki—— of England had undertaken in his *own Right*, to support the Parliament in what he calls *Theirs*, and as the good people of this country are grievously oppressed by the combination, they have an undoubted privilege to inquire into the pretensions of both, and equally to reject the usurpation of either.

In the following sheets, the author hath studiously avoided every thing which is personal among ourselves. Compliments as well as censure to individuals make no part thereof. The wise, and the worthy, need not the triumph of a pamphlet; and those whose sentiments are injudicious, or unfriendly, will cease of themselves unless too much pains are bestowed upon their conversion.

The cause of America is in a great measure the cause of all mankind. Many circumstances hath, and will arise, which are not local, but universal, and through which the principles of all Lovers of Mankind are affected, and in the Event of which, their Affections are interested. The laying a Country desolate with Fire and Sword, declaring War against the natural rights of all Mankind, and extirpating the Defenders thereof from the Face of the Earth, is the Concern of every Man to whom Nature hath given the Power of feeling; of which Class, regardless of Party Censure, is the

AUTHOR.

P.S. The Publication of this new Edition hath been delayed, with a View of taking notice (had it been necessary) of any Attempt to refute the Doctrine of Independance: As no Answer hath yet appeared, it is now presumed that none will, the Time needful for getting such a Performance ready for the Public being considerably past.

Who the Author of this Production is, is wholly unnecessary to the Public, as the Object for Attention is the *Doctrine itself*, not the *Man*. Yet it may not be unnecessary to say, That he is unconnected with any Party, and under no sort of Influence public or private, but the influence of reason and principle.

Philadelphia, February 14, 1776.

COMMON SENSE

OF THE ORIGIN AND DESIGN OF GOVERNMENT IN GENERAL. WITH CONCISE REMARKS ON THE ENGLISH CONSTITUTION.

SOME writers have so confounded society with government, as to leave little or no distinction between them; whereas they are not only different, but have different origins. Society is produced by our wants, and government by our wickedness; the former promotes our happiness *positively* by uniting our affections, the latter *negatively* by restraining our vices. The one encourages intercourse, the other creates distinctions. The first is a patron, the last a punisher.

Society in every state is a blessing, but government even in its best state, is but a necessary evil; in its worst state an intolerable one; for when we suffer, or are exposed to the same miseries *by a government*, which we might expect in a country *without government*, our calamities is heightened by reflecting that we furnish the means by which we suffer. Government, like dress, is the badge of lost innocence; the palaces of kings are built upon the ruins of the bowers of paradise. For were the impulses of conscience clear, uniform, and irresistibly obeyed, man would need no other lawgiver; but that not being the case, he finds it necessary to surrender up a part of his property to furnish means for the protection of the rest; and this he is induced to do by the same prudence which in every other case advises him, out of two evils to choose the least. *Wherefore*, security being the true design and end of government, it unanswerably follows that whatever *form* thereof appears most likely to ensure it to us, with the least expense and greatest benefit, is preferable to all others.

In order to gain a clear and just idea of the design and end of government, let us suppose a small number of persons settled in some sequestered part of the earth, unconnected with the rest; they will then represent the first peopling of any country, or of the world. In this state of natural liberty, society will be their first thought. A thousand motives will excite them thereto, the strength of one man is so unequal to his wants, and his mind so unfitted for perpetual solitude, that he is soon obliged to seek assistance and relief of another, who in his turn requires the same. Four or five united would be able to raise a tolerable dwelling in the midst of a wilderness, but *one* man might labour out the common period of life without accomplishing any thing; when he had felled his timber he could not remove it, nor erect it after it was removed; hunger in the mean time would urge him from his work, and every different want call him a different way. Disease, nay even misfortune, would be death; for though neither might be mortal, yet either would disable him from living, and reduce him to a state in which he might rather be said to perish than to die.

Thus necessity, like a gravitating power, would soon form our newly arrived emigrants into society, the reciprocal blessings of which, would supercede, and render the obligations of law and government unnecessary while they remained perfectly just to each other; but as nothing but heaven is impregnable to vice, it will unavoidably happen, that in proportion as they surmount the first difficulties of emigration, which bound them together in a common cause, they will begin to relax in their duty and attachment to each other; and this remissness, will point out the necessity, of establishing some form of government to supply the defect of moral virtue.

Some convenient tree will afford them a State-House, under the branches of which the whole colony may assemble to deliberate on public matters. It is more than probable that their first laws will have the title only of REGULATIONS, and be enforced by no other penalty than public disesteem. In this first parliament every man, by natural right will have a seat.

But as the colony increases, the public concerns will increase likewise, and the distance at which the members may be separated, will render it too inconvenient for all of them to meet on every occasion as at first, when their number was small, their habitations near, and the public concerns few and trifling. This will point out the convenience of their consenting to leave the legislative part to be managed by a select number chosen from the whole body, who are supposed to have the same concerns at stake which those have who appointed them, and who will act in the same manner as the whole body would act were they present. If the colony continue increasing, it will become necessary to augment the number of the representatives, and that the interest of every part of the colony may be attended to, it will be found best to divide the whole into convenient parts, each part sending its proper number; and that the *elected* might never form to themselves an interest separate from the *electors*, prudence will point out the propriety of having elections often; because as the *elected* might by that means return and mix again with the general body of the *electors* in a few months, their fidelity to the public will be secured by the prudent reflection of not making a rod for themselves. And as this frequent interchange will establish a common interest with every part of the community, they will mutually and naturally support each other, and on this (not on the unmeaning name of king) depends the *strength of government, and the happiness of the governed.*

Here then is the origin and rise of government; namely, a mode rendered necessary by the inability of moral virtue to govern the world; here too is the design and end of government, viz. freedom and security. And however our eyes may be dazzled with snow, or our ears deceived by sound; however prejudice may warp our wills, or interest darken our understanding, the simple voice of nature and reason will say, it is right.

I draw my idea of the form of government from a principle in nature, which no art can overturn, viz. that the more simple any thing is, the less liable it is to be disordered, and the easier repaired when disordered; and with this maxim in view, I offer a few remarks on the so much boasted constitution of England. That it was noble for the dark and slavish times in which it was erected is granted. When the world was over-run with tyranny the least remove therefrom was a glorious rescue. But that it is imperfect, subject to convulsions, and incapable of producing what it seems to promise, is easily demonstrated.

Absolute governments (tho' the disgrace of human nature) have this advantage with them, that they are simple; if the people suffer, they know the head from which their suffering springs, know likewise the remedy, and are not bewildered by a variety of causes and cures. But the constitution of England is so exceedingly complex, that the nation may suffer for years together without being able to discover in which part the fault lies, some will say in one and some in another, and every political physician will advise a different medicine.

I know it is difficult to get over local or long standing prejudices, yet if we will suffer ourselves to examine the component parts of the English constitution, we shall find them to be the base remains of two ancient tyrannies, compounded with some new republican materials.

First. — The remains of monarchical tyranny in the person of the king.

Secondly. — The remains of aristocratical tyranny in the persons of the peers.

Thirdly. — The new republican materials, in the persons of the commons, on whose virtue depends the freedom of England.

The two first, by being hereditary, are independent of the people; wherefore in a *constitutional sense* they contribute nothing towards the freedom of the state.

To say that the constitution of England is a *union* of three powers reciprocally *checking* each other, is farcical, either the words have no meaning, or they are flat contradictions.

To say that the commons is a check upon the king, presupposes two things.

First. — That the king is not to be trusted without being looked after, or in other words, that a thirst for absolute power is the natural disease of monarchy.

Secondly. — That the commons, by being appointed for that purpose, are either wiser or more worthy of confidence than the crown.

But as the same constitution which gives the commons a power to check the king by withholding the supplies, gives afterwards the king a power to check the commons, by empowering him to reject their other bills; it again supposes that the king is wiser than those whom it has already supposed to be wiser than him. A mere absurdity!

There is something exceedingly ridiculous in the composition of monarchy; it first excludes a man from the means of information, yet empowers him to act in cases where the highest judgment is required. The state of a king shuts him from the world, yet the business of a king requires him to know it thoroughly; wherefore the different parts, unnaturally opposing and destroying each other, prove the whole character to be absurd and useless.

Some writers have explained the English constitution thus; the king, say they, is one, the people another; the peers are an house in behalf of the king; the commons in behalf of the people; but this hath all the distinctions of a house divided against itself; and though the expressions be pleasantly arranged, yet when examined they appear idle and ambiguous; and it will always happen, that the nicest construction that words are capable of, when applied to the description of some thing which either cannot exist, or is too incomprehensible to be within the compass of description, will be words of sound only, and though they may amuse the ear, they cannot inform the mind, for this explanation includes a previous question, viz. *How came the king by a power which the people are afraid to trust, and always obliged to check?* Such a power could not be the gift of a wise people, neither can any power, *which needs checking*, be from God; yet the provision, which the constitution makes, supposes such a power to exist.

But the provision is unequal to the task; the means either cannot or will not accomplish the end, and the whole affair is a *felo de se*; for as the greater weight will always carry up the less, and as all the wheels of a machine are put in motion by one, it only remains to know which power in the constitution has the most weight, for that will govern; and though the others, or a part of them, may clog, or, as the phrase is, check the rapidity of its motion, yet so long as they cannot stop it, their endeavours will be ineffectual; the first moving power will at last have its way, and what it wants in speed is supplied by time.

That the crown is this overbearing part in the English constitution needs not be mentioned, and that it derives its whole consequence merely from being the giver of places and pensions is self-evident, wherefore, though we have been wise enough to shut and lock a door against absolute monarchy, we at the same time have been foolish enough to put the crown in possession of the key.

The prejudice of Englishmen, in favour of their own government by king, lords, and commons, arises as much or more from national pride than reason. Individuals are undoubtedly safer in England than in some other countries, but the *will* of the king is as much the *law* of the land in Britain as in France, with this difference, that instead of proceeding directly from his mouth, it is handed to the people under the most formidable shape of an act of parliament. For the fate of Charles the First, hath only made kings more subtle — not more just.

Wherefore, laying aside all national pride and prejudice in favour of modes and forms, the plain truth is, that *it is wholly owing to the constitution of the people, and not to the constitution of the government* that the crown is not as oppressive in England as in Turkey.

An inquiry into the *constitutional errors* in the English form of government is at this time highly necessary; for as we are never in a proper condition of doing justice to others, while we continue under the influence of some leading partiality, so neither are we capable of doing it to ourselves while we remain fettered by any obstinate prejudice. And as a man, who is attached to a prostitute, is unfitted to choose or judge of a wife, so any prepossession in favour of a rotten constitution of government will disable us from discerning a good one.

OF MONARCHY AND HEREDITARY SUCCESSION.

MANKIND being originally equals in the order of creation, the equality could only be destroyed by some subsequent circumstance; the distinctions of rich, and poor, may in a great measure be accounted for, and that without having recourse to the harsh, ill-sounding names of oppression and avarice. Oppression is often the *consequence*, but seldom or never the *means* of riches; and though avarice will preserve a man from being necessitously poor, it generally makes him too timorous to be wealthy.

But thre is another and great distinction for which no truly natural or religious reason can be assigned, and that is, the distinction of men into KINGS and SUBJECTS. Male and female are the distinctions of nature, good and bad the distinctions of heaven; but how a race of men came into the world so exalted above the rest, and distinguished like some new species, is worth enquiring into, and whether they are the means of happiness or of misery to mankind.

In the early ages of the world, according to the scripture chronology, there were no kings; the consequence of which was there were no wars; it is the pride of kings which throw mankind into confusion. Holland without a king hath enjoyed more peace for this last century than any of the monarchical governments in Europe. Antiquity favors the same remark; for the quiet and rural lives of the first patriarchs hath a happy something in them, which vanishes away when we come to the history of Jewish royalty.

Government by kings was first introduced into the world by the Heathens, from whom the children of Israel copied the custom. It was the most prosperous invention the Devil ever set on foot for the promotion of idolatry. The Heathens paid divine honors to their deceased kings, and the christian world hath improved on the plan by doing the same to their living ones. How impious is the title of *sacred majesty* applied to a worm, who in the midst of his splendor is crumbling into dust.

As the exalting one man so greatly above the rest cannot be justified on the equal rights of nature, so neither can it be defended on the authority of scripture; for the will of the Almighty, as declared by Gideon and the prophet Samuel, expressly disapproves of government by kings. All anti-monarchical parts of scripture have been very smoothly glossed over in monarchical governments, but they undoubtedly merit the attention of countries which have their governments yet to form. 'Render unto Cæsar the things which are Cæsar's' is the scriptural doctrine of courts, yet it is no support of monarchical government, for the Jews at that time were without a king, and in a state of vassalage to the Romans.

Near three thousand years passed away from the Mosaic account of the creation, till the Jews under a national delusion requested a king. Till then their form of government (except in extraordinary cases, where the Almighty interposed) was a kind of republic administered by a judge and the elders of the tribes. Kings they had none, and it was held sinful to acknowledge any being under that title but the Lord of Hosts. And when a man seriously reflects on the idolatrous homage which is paid to the persons of Kings, he need not wonder, that the Almighty, ever jealous of his honor, should disapprove of a form of government which so impiously invades the prerogative of heaven.

Monarchy is ranked in scripture as one of the sins of the Jews, for which a curse in reserve is denounced against them. The history of that transaction is worth attending to.

The children of Israel being oppressed by the Midianites, Gideon marched against them with a small army, and victory, thro' the divine interposition decided in his favour. The Jews elate with success, and attributing it to the generalship of Gideon, proposed making him a king, saying, *Rule thou over us, thou and thy son and thy son's son.* Here was temptation in its fullest extent; not a kingdom only, but an hereditary one, but Gideon in the piety of his soul replied, *I will not rule over you, neither shall my son rule over you,* THE LORD SHALL RULE OVER YOU. Words need not be more explicit; Gideon doth not *decline* the honor but denieth their right to give it; neither doth he compliment them with invented declarations of his thanks, but in the positive stile of a prophet charges them with disaffection to their proper sovereign, the King of Heaven.

About one hundred and thirty years after this, they fell again into the same error. The hankering which the Jews had for the idolatrous customs of the Heathens, is something exceedingly unaccountable; but so it was, that laying hold of the misconduct of Samuel's two sons, who were entrusted with some secular concerns, they came in an abrupt and clamourous manner to Samuel, saying, *Behold thou art old, and thy sons walk not in thy ways, now make us a king to judge us like all the other nations.* And here we cannot but observe that their motives were bad, viz. that they might be *like* unto other nations, i.e. the Heathens, whereas their true glory laid in being as much *unlike* them as possible. *But the thing displeased Samuel when they said, give us a king to judge us; and Samuel prayed unto the Lord, and the Lord said unto Samuel, Hearken unto the voice of the people in all that they say unto thee, for they have not rejected thee, but they have rejected me,* THAT I SHOULD NOT REIGN OVER THEM. *According to all the works which they have done since the day that I brought them up out of Egypt, even unto this day; wherewith they have forsaken me and served other Gods; so do they also unto thee. Now therefore hearken unto their voice, howbeit, protest solemnly unto them and shew them the manner of the king that shall reign over them, i.e.* not of any particular king, but the general manner of the kings of the earth, whom Israel was so eagerly copying after. And notwithstanding the great distance of time and difference of manners, the character is still in fashion. *And Samuel told all the words of the Lord unto the people, that asked of him a king. And he said, This shall be the manner of the king that shall reign over you; he will take your sons and appoint them for himself for his chariots, and to be his horsemen, and some shall run before his chariots* (this description agrees with the present mode of impressing men) *and he will appoint him captains over thousands and captains over fifties, and will set them to ear his ground and to reap his harvest, and to make his instruments of war, and instruments of his chariots; and he will take your daughters to be confectionaries, and to be cooks and to be bak-*

ers (this describes the expence and luxury as well as the oppression of kings) *and he will take your fields and your olive yards, even the best of them, and give them to his servants; and he will take the tenth of your seed, and of your vineyards, and give them to his officers and to his servants* (by which we see that bribery, corruption, and favoritism are the standing vices of kings) *and he will take the tenth of your men servants, and your maid servants, and your goodliest young men and your asses, and put them to his work; and he will take the tenth of your sheep, and ye shall be his servants, and ye shall cry out in that day because of your king which ye shall have chosen,* AND THE LORD WILL NOT HEAR YOU IN THAT DAY. This accounts for the continuation of monarchy; neither do the characters of the few good kings which have lived since, either sanctify the title, or blot out the sinfulness of the origin; the high encomium given of David takes no notice of him *officially as a king*, but only as a *man* after God's own heart. *Nevertheless the People refused to obey the voice of Samuel, and they said, Nay, but we will have a king over us, that we may be like all the nations, and that our king may judge us, and go out before us and fight our battles.* Samuel continued to reason with them, but to no purpose; he set before them their ingratitude, but all would not avail; and seeing them fully bent on their folly, he cried out, *I will call unto the Lord, and he shall send thunder and rain* (which then was a punishment, being the time of wheat harvest) *that ye may perceive and see that your wickedness is great which ye have done in the sight of the Lord,* IN ASKING YOU A KING. *So Samuel called unto the Lord, and the Lord sent thunder and rain that day, and all the people greatly feared the Lord and Samuel. And all the people said unto Samuel, Pray for thy servants unto the Lord thy God that we die not, for* WE HAVE ADDED UNTO OUR SINS THIS EVIL, TO ASK A KING. These portions of scripture are direct and positive. They admit of no equivocal construction. That the Almighty hath here entered his protest against monarchical government is true, or the scripture is false. And a man hath good reason to believe that there is as much of king-craft, as priest-craft in withholding the scripture from the public in Popish countries. For monarchy in every instance is the Popery of government.

To the evil of monarchy we have added that of hereditary succession; and as the first is a degradation and lessening of ourselves, so the second, claimed as a matter of right, is an insult and an imposition on posterity. For all men being originally equals, no *one* by *birth* could have a right to set up his own family in perpetual preference to all others for ever, and though himself might deserve *some* decent degree of honors of his contemporaries, yet his descendants might be far too unworthy to inherit them. One of the strongest *natural* proofs of the folly of hereditary right in kings, is, that nature disapproves it, otherwise she would not so frequently turn it into ridicule by giving mankind an *ass for a lion*.

Secondly, as no man at first could possess any other public honors than were bestowed upon him, so the givers of those honors could have no power to give away the right of posterity, and though they might say 'We choose you for *our* head,' they could not, without manifest injustice to their children, say 'that your children and your children's children shall reign over *ours* for ever.' Because such an unwise, unjust, unnatural compact might (perhaps) in the next succession put them under the government of a rogue or a fool. Most wise men, in their private sentiments, have ever treated hereditary right with contempt; yet it is one of those evils, which when once established is not easily removed; many submit from fear, others from superstition, and the more powerful part shares with the king the plunder of the rest.

This is supposing the present race of kings in the world to have had an honourable origin; whereas it is more than probable, that could we take off the dark covering of antiquity, and trace them to their first rise, that we should find the first of them nothing better than the principal ruffian of some restless gang, whose savage manners or pre-eminence in subtilty obtained him the title of chief among plunderers; and who by increasing in power, and extending his depredations, over-awed the quiet and defenceless to purchase their safety by frequent contributions. Yet his electors could have no idea of giving hereditary right to his descendants, because such a perpetual exclusion of themselves was incompatible with the free and unrestrained principles they professed to live by. Wherefore, hereditary succession in the early ages of monarchy could not take place as a matter of claim, but as something casual or complimental; but as few or no records were extant in those days, the traditionary history stuffed with fables, it was very easy, after the lapse of a few generations, to trump up some superstitious tale conveniently timed, Mahomet like, to cram hereditary right down the throats of the vulgar. Perhaps the disorders which threatened, or seemed to threaten on the decease of a leader and the choice of a new one (for elections among ruffians could not be very orderly) induced many at first to favor hereditary pretensions; by which means it happened, as it hath happened since, that what at first was submitted to as a convenience, was afterwards claimed as a right.

England, since the conquest, hath known some few good monarchs, but groaned beneath a much larger number of bad ones, yet no man in his senses can say that their claim under William the Conqueror is a very honorable one. A French bastard landing with an armed banditti, and establishing himself king of England against the consent of the natives, is in plain terms a very paltry rascally original. — It certainly hath no divinity in it. However it is needless to spend much time in exposing the folly of hereditary right, if there are any so weak as to believe it, let them promiscuously worship the ass and the lion, and welcome. I shall neither copy their humility, nor disturb their devotion.

Yet I should be glad to ask how they suppose kings came at first? The question admits but of three answers, viz. either by lot, by election, or by usurpation. If the first king was taken by lot, it establishes a precedent for the next, which excludes hereditary succession. Saul was by lot yet the succession was not hereditary, neither does it appear from that transaction there was any intention it ever should. If the first king of any country was by election, that likewise establishes a precedent for the next; for to say, that the *right* of all future generations is taken away, by the act of the first electors, in their choice not only of a king, but of a family of kings for ever, hath no parallel in or out of scripture but the doctrine of original sin, which supposes the free will of all men lost in Adam; and from such comparison, and it will admit of no other, hereditary succession can derive no glory. For as in Adam all sinned, and as in the first electors all men obeyed; as in the one all mankind were subjected to Satan, and in the other to Sovereignty; as our innocence was lost in the first, and our authority in the last; and as both disable us from re-assuming some former state and privilege, it unanswerably follows that original sin and hereditary succession are parallels. Dishonourable rank! Inglorious connexion! Yet the most subtile sophist cannot produce a juster simile.

As to usurpation, no man will be so hardy as to defend it; and that William the Conqueror was an usurper is a fact not to be contradicted. The plain truth is, that the antiquity of English monarchy will not bear looking into.

But it is not so much the absurdity as the evil of hereditary succession which concerns mankind. Did it ensure a race of good and wise men it would have the seal of divine authority, but as it opens a door to the *foolish*, the *wicked*, and the *improper*, it hath in it the nature of oppression. Men who look upon themselves born to reign, and others to obey, soon grow insolent; selected from the rest of mankind their minds are early poisoned by importance; and the world they act in differs so materially from the world at large, that they have but little opportunity of knowing its true interests, and when they succeed to the government are frequently the most ignorant and unfit of any throughout the dominions.

Another evil which attends hereditary succession is, that the throne is subject to be possessed by a minor at any age; all which time the regency, acting under the cover of a king, have every opportunity and inducement to betray their trust. The same national misfortune happens, when a king worn out with age and infirmity enters the last stage of human weakness. In both these cases the public becomes a prey to every miscreant, who can tamper successfully with the follies either of age or infancy.

The most plausible plea, which hath ever been offered in favour of hereditary succession, is, that it preserves a nation from civil wars; and were this true, it would be weighty; whereas, it is the most barefaced falsity ever imposed upon mankind. The whole history of England disowns the fact. Thirty kings and two minors have reigned in that distracted kingdom since the conquest, in which time there have been (including the Revolution) no less than eight civil wars and nineteen rebellions. Wherefore instead of making for peace, it makes against it, and destroys the very foundation it seems to stand upon.

The contest for monarchy and succession, between the houses of York and Lancaster, laid England in a scene of blood for many years. Twelve pitched battles, besides skirmishes and sieges, were fought between Henry and Edward. Twice was Henry prisoner to Edward, who in his turn was prisoner to Henry. And so uncertain is the fate of war and the temper of a nation, when nothing but personal matters are the ground of a quarrel, that Henry was taken in triumph from a prison to a palace, and Edward obliged to fly from a palace to a foreign land; yet, as sudden transitions of temper are seldom lasting, Henry in his turn was driven from the throne, and Edward recalled to succeed him. The parliament always following the strongest side.

This contest began in the reign of Henry the Sixth, and was not entirely extinguished till Henry the Seventh, in whom the families were united. Including a period of 67 years, viz. from 1422 to 1489.

In short, monarchy and succession have laid (not this or that kingdom only) but the world in blood and ashes. 'Tis a form of government which the word of God bears testimony against, and blood will attend it.

If we inquire into the business of a king, we shall find that in some countries they may have none; and after sauntering away their lives without pleasure to themselves or advantage to the nation, withdraw from the scene, and leave their successors to tread the same idle round. In absolute monarchies the whole weight of business civil and military, lies on the king; the children of Israel in their request for a king, urged this plea 'that he may judge us, and go out before us and fight our battles.' But in countries where he is neither a judge nor a general, as in E——d, a man would be puzzled to know what is his business.

The nearer any government approaches to a republic the less business there is for a king. It is somewhat difficult to find a proper name for the government of E——d. Sir William Meredith calls it a republic; but in its present state it is unworthy of the name, because the corrupt influence of the crown, by having all the places in its disposal, hath so effectually swallowed up the power, and eaten out the virtue of the house of commons (the republican part in the constitution) that the government of England is nearly as monarchical as that of France or Spain. Men fall out with names without understanding them. For it is the republican and not the monarchical part of the constitution of England which Englishmen glory in, viz. the liberty of choosing an house of commons from out of their own body — and it is easy to see that when republican virtue fails, slavery ensues. Why is the constitution of E——d sickly, but because monarchy hath poisoned the republic, the crown hath engrossed the commons?

In England a k—— hath little more to do than to make war and give away places; which, in plain terms, is to impoverish the nation and set it together by the ears. A pretty business indeed for a man to be allowed eight hundred thousand sterling a year for, and worshipped into the bargain! Of more worth is one honest man to society, and in the sight of God, than all the crowned ruffians that ever lived.

THOUGHTS ON THE PRESENT STATE OF
AMERICAN AFFAIRS.

In the following pages I offer nothing more than simple facts, plain arguments, and common sense; and have no other preliminaries to settle with the reader, than that he will divest himself of prejudice and prepossession, and suffer his reason and his feelings to determine for themselves; that he will put *on*, or rather that he will not put *off*, the true character of a man, and generously enlarge his views beyond the present day.

Volumes have been written on the subject of the struggle between England and America. Men of all ranks have embarked in the controversy, from different motives, and with various designs; but all have been ineffectual, and the period of debate is closed. Arms, as the last resource, decide the contest; the appeal was the choice of the king, and the continent has accepted the challenge.

It hath been reported of the late Mr. Pelham (who tho' an able minister was not without his faults) that on his being attacked in the house of commons, on the score, that his measures were only of a temporary kind, replied, '*they will last my time.*' Should a thought so fatal and unmanly possess the colonies in the present contest, the name of ancestors will be remembered by future generations with detestation.

The sun never shined on a cause of greater worth. 'Tis not the affair of a city, a country, a province, or a kingdom, but of a conti-nent — of at least one eighth part of the habitable globe. 'Tis not the concern of a day, a year, or an age; posterity are virtually involved in the contest, and will be more or less affected, even to the end of time, by the proceedings now. Now is the seed time of continental union, faith and honor. The least fracture now will be like a name engraved with the point of a pin on the tender rind of a young oak; the wound will enlarge with the tree, and posterity read in it full grown characters.

By referring the matter from argument to arms, a new æra for politics is struck; a new method of thinking hath arisen. All plans, proposals, &c. prior to the nineteenth of April, *i.e.* to the commencement of hostilities, are like the almanacks of the last year; which, though proper then, are superceded and useless now. Whatever was advanced by the advocates on either side of the question then, terminated in one and the same point, viz. a union with Great Britain; the only difference between the parties was the method of effecting it; the one proposing force, the other friendship; but it hath so far happened that the first hath failed, and the second hath withdrawn her influence.

As much hath been said of the advantages of reconciliation, which, like an agreeable dream, hath passed away and left us as we were, it is but right, that we should examine the contrary side of the argument, and inquire into some of the many material injuries which these colonies sustain, and always will sustain, by being connected with, and dependant on Great Britain. To examine that connexion and dependance, on the principles of nature and common sense, to see what we have to trust to, if separated, and what we are to expect, if dependant.

I have heard it asserted by some, that as America hath flourished under her former connexion with Great-Britain, that the same connexion is necessary towards her future happiness, and will always have the same effect. Nothing can be more fallacious than this kind of argument. We may as well assert, that because a child has thrived upon milk, that it is never to have meat; or that the first twenty years of our lives is to become a precedent for the next twenty. But even this is admitting more than is true, for I answer roundly, that America would have flourished as much, and probably much more, had no European power had anything to do with her. The commerce by which she hath enriched herself are the necessaries of life, and will always have a market while eating is the custom of Europe.

But she has protected us, say some. That she hath engrossed us is true, and defended the continent at our expence as well as her own is admitted, and she would have defended Turkey from the same motive, viz. the sake of trade and dominion.

Alas, we have been long led away by ancient prejudices, and made large sacrifices to superstition. We have boasted the protection of Great-Britain, without considering, that her motive was *interest* not *attachment*; that she did not protect us from *our enemies* on *our account*, but from *her enemies* on *her own account*, from those who had no quarrel with us on any *other account*, and who will always be our enemies on the *same account*. Let Britain wave her pretensions to the continent, or the continent throw off the dependance, and we should be at peace with France and Spain, were they at war with Britain. The miseries of Hanover last war ought to warn us against connexions.

It hath lately been asserted in parliament, that the colonies have no relation to each other but through the parent country, *i.e.* that Pennsylvania and the Jerseys, and so on for the rest, are sister colonies by the way of England; this is certainly a very round-about way of proving relationship, but it is the nearest and only true way of proving enemyship, if I may so call it. France and Spain never were, nor perhaps ever will be our enemies as *Americans*, but as our being the *subjects of Great Britain*.

But Britain is the parent country, say some. Then the more shame upon her conduct. Even brutes do not devour their young, nor savages make war upon their families; wherefore the assertion, if true, turns to her reproach; but it happens not to be true, or only partly so, and the phrase *parent* or *mother country* hath been jesuitically adopted by the —— and his parasites, with a low papistical design of gaining an unfair bias on the credulous weakness of our minds. Europe, and not England, is the parent country of America. This new world hath been the asylum for the persecuted lovers of civil and religious liberty from *every part* of Europe. Hither have they fled, not from the tender embraces of the mother, but from the cruelty of the monster; and it is so far true of England, that the same tyranny which drove the first emigrants from home, pursues their descendants still.

In this extensive quarter of the globe, we forget the narrow limits of three hundred and sixty miles (the extent of England) and carry our friendship on a larger scale; we claim brotherhood with eve-European christian, and triumph in the generosity of the sentiment.

It is pleasant to observe by what regular gradations we surmount the force of local prejudices, as we enlarge our acquaintance with the world. A man born in any town in England divided into parishes, will naturally associate most with his fellow parishioners (because their interests in many cases will be common) and distinguish him by the name of *neighbour*; if he meet him but a few miles from home, he drops the narrow idea of a street, and salutes him by the name of *townsman*; if he travels out of the county and meet him in any other, he forgets the minor divisions of street and town, and calls him *countryman*; i.e. *countyman*; but if in their foreign excursions they should associate in France, or any other part of *Europe*, their local remembrance would be enlarged into that of *Englishmen*. And by a just parity of reasoning, all Europeans meeting in America, or any other quarter of the globe, are *countrymen*; for England, Holland, Germany, or Sweden, when compared with the whole, stand in the same places on the larger scale, which the divisions of street, town, and county do on the smaller ones; distinctions too limited for continental minds. Not one third of the inhabitants, even of this province, are of English descent. Wherefore I reprobate the phrase of parent or mother country applied to England only, as being false, selfish, narrow and ungenerous.

But admitting that we were all of English descent, what does it amount to? Nothing. Britain, being now an open enemy, extinguishes every other name and title: And to say that reconciliation is our duty, is truly farcical. The first king of England, of the present line (William the Conqueror) was a Frenchman, and half the peers of England are descendants from the same country; wherefore by the same method of reasoning, England ought to be governed by France.

Much hath been said of the united strength of Britain and the colonies, that in conjunction they might bid defiance to the world. But this is mere presumption; the fate of war is uncertain, neither do the expressions mean any thing; for this continent would never suffer itself to be drained of inhabitants to support the British arms in either Asia, Africa, or Europe.

Besides, what have we to do with setting the world at defiance? Our plan is commerce, and that, well attended to, will secure us the peace and friendship of all Europe; because it is the interest of all Europe to have America a *free port*. Her trade will always be a protection, and her barrenness of gold and silver secure her from invaders.

I challenge the warmest advocate for reconciliation, to shew, a single advantage that this continent can reap, by being connected with Great Britain. I repeat the challenge, not a single advantage is derived. Our corn will fetch its price in any market in Europe, and our imported goods must be paid for buy them where we will.

But the injuries and disadvantages which we sustain by that connection, are without number; and our duty to mankind at large, as well as to ourselves, instruct us to renounce the alliance: Because, any submission to, or dependance on Great Britain, tends directly to involve this continent in European wars and quarrels; and set us at variance with nations, who would otherwise seek our friendship, and against whom, we have neither anger nor complaint. As Europe is our market for trade, we ought to form no partial connection with any part of it. It is the true interest of America to steer clear of European contentions, which she never can do, while by her dependance on Britain, she is made the make-weight in the scale of British politics.

Europe is too thickly planted with kingdoms to be long at peace, and whenever a war breaks out between England and any foreign power, the trade of America goes to ruin, *because of her connection with Britain.* The next war may not turn out like the last, and should it not, the advocates for reconciliation now will be wishing for separation then, because, neutrality in that case, would be a safer convoy than a man of war. Every thing that is right or natural pleads for separation. The blood of the slain, the weeping voice of nature cries, 'TIS TIME TO PART. Even the distance at which the Almighty hath placed England and America, is a strong and natural proof, that the authority of the one, over the other, was never the design of Heaven. The time likewise at which the continent was discovered, adds weight to the argument, and the manner in which it was peopled encreases the force of it. The reformation was preceded by the discovery of America, as if the Almighty graciously meant to open a sanctuary to the persecuted in future years, when home should afford neither friendship nor safety.

The authority of Great-Britain over this continent, is a form of government, which sooner or later must have an end: And a serious mind can draw no true pleasure by looking forward, under the painful and positive conviction, that what he calls 'the present constitution' is merely temporary. As parents, we can have no joy, knowing that *this government* is not sufficiently lasting to ensure any thing which we may bequeath to posterity: And by a plain method of argument, as we are running the next generation into debt, we ought to do the work of it, otherwise we use them meanly and pitifully. In order to discover the line of our duty rightly, we should take our children in our hand, and fix our station a few years farther into life; that eminence will present a prospect, which a few present fears and prejudices conceal from our sight.

Though I would carefully avoid giving unnecessary offence, yet I am inclined to believe, that all those who espouse the doctrine of reconciliation, may be included within the following descriptions. Interested men, who are not to be trusted; weak men who *cannot* see; prejudiced men who *will not* see; and a certain set of moderate men, who think better of the European world than it deserves; and this last class by an ill-judged deliberation, will be the cause of more calamities to this continent than all the other three.

It is the good fortune of many to live distant from the scene of sorrow; the evil is not sufficiently brought to *their* doors to make *them* feel the precariousness with which all American property is possessed. But let our imaginations transport us for a few moments to Boston, that seat of wretchedness will teach us wisdom, and instruct us for ever to renounce a power in whom we can have no trust. The inhabitants of that unfortunate city, who but a few months ago were in ease and affluence, have now no other alternative than to stay and starve, or turn out to beg. Endangered by the fire of their friends if they continue within the city, and plundered by the soldiery if they leave it. In their present condition they are prisoners without the hope of redemption, and in a general attack for their relief, they would be exposed to the fury of both armies.

Men of passive tempers look somewhat lightly over the offences of Britain, and, still hoping for the best, are apt to call out, '*Come we shall be friends again for all this.*' But examine the passions and feelings of mankind. Bring the doctrine of reconciliation to the touchstone of nature, and then tell me, whether you can hereafter love, honour, and faithfully serve the power that hath carried fire and sword into your land? If you cannot do all these, then are you only deceiving yourselves, and by your delay bringing ruin upon posterity. Your future connection with Britain, whom you can neither love nor honour, will be forced and unnatural, and being formed only on the plan of present convenience, will in a little time fall into a relapse more wretched than the first. But if you say, you can still pass the violations over, then I ask, Hath your house been burnt? Hath your property been destroyed before your face? Are your wife and children destitute of a bed to lie on, or bread to live on? Have you lost a parent or a child by their hands, and yourself the ruined and wretched survivor? If you have not, then are you not a judge of those who have. But if you have, and can still shake hands with the murderers, then are you unworthy the name of husband, father, friend, or lover, and whatever may be your rank or title in life, you have the heart of a coward, and the spirit of a sycophant.

This is not inflaming or exaggerating matters, but trying them by those feelings and affections which nature justifies, and without which, we should be incapable of discharging the social duties of life, or enjoying the felicities of it. I mean not to exhibit horror for the purpose of provoking revenge, but to awaken us from fatal and unmanly slumbers, that we may pursue determinately some fixed object. It is not in the power of Britain or of Europe to conquer America, if she do not conquer herself by *delay* and *timidity*. The present winter is worth an age if rightly employed, but if lost or neglected, the whole continent will partake of the misfortune; and there is no punishment which that man will not deserve, be he who, or what, or where he will, that may be the means of sacrificing a season so precious and useful.

It is repugnant to reason, to the universal order of things, to all examples from the former ages, to suppose, that this continent can longer remain subject to any external power. The most sanguine in Britain does not think so. The utmost stretch of human wisdom cannot, at this time compass a plan short of separation, which can promise the continent even a year's security. Reconciliation is a fala-cious dream. Nature hath deserted the connexion, and Art cannot supply her place. For, as Milton wisely expresses, 'never can true rec-oncilement grow where wounds of deadly hate have pierced so deep.'

Every quiet method for peace hath been ineffectual. Our prayers have been rejected with disdain; and only tended to convince us, that nothing flatters vanity, or confirms obstinancy in Kings more than repeated petitioning — and nothing hath contributed more than that very measure to make the Kings of Europe absolute: Witness Denmark and Sweden. Wherefore since nothing but blows will do, for God's sake, let us come to a final separation, and not leave the next generation to be cutting throats, under the violated unmeaning names of parent and child.

To say, they will never attempt it again is idle and visionary, we thought so at the repeal of the stamp-act, yet a year or two unde-ceived us; as well we may suppose that nations, which have been once defeated, will never renew the quarrel.

As to government matters, it is not in the power of Britain to do this continent justice: The business of it will soon be too weighty, and intricate, to be managed with any tolerable degree of conven-ience, by a power, so distant from us, and so very ignorant of us; for if they cannot conquer us, they cannot govern us. To be always run-ning three or four thousand miles with a tale or a petition, waiting four or five months for an answer, which when obtained requires five or six more to explain it in, will in a few years be looked upon as folly and childishness — There was a time when it was proper, and there is a proper time for it to cease.

Small islands not capable of protecting themselves, are the proper objects for kingdoms to take under their care; but there is something very absurd, in supposing a continent to be perpetually governed by an island. In no instance hath nature made the satellite larger than its primary planet, and as England and America, with respect to each other, reverses the common order of nature, it is evident they belong to different systems: England to Europe, America to itself.

I am not induced by motives of pride, party, or resentment to espouse the doctrine of separation and independence; I am clearly, positively, and conscientiously persuaded that it is the true interest of this continent to be so; that every thing short of *that* is mere patchwork, that it can afford no lasting felicity, — that it is leaving the sword to our children, and shrinking back at a time, when, a little more, a little farther, would have rendered this continent the glory of the earth.

As Britain hath not manifested the least inclination towards a compromise, we may be assured that no terms can be obtained worthy the acceptance of the continent, or any ways equal to the expence of blood and treasure we have been already put to.

The object contended for, ought always to bear some just proportion to the expence. The removal of N——, or the whole detestable junto, is a matter unworthy the millions we have expended. A temporary stoppage of trade, was an inconvenience, which would have sufficiently ballanced the repeal of all the acts complained of, had such repeals been obtained; but if the whole continent must take up arms, if every man must be a soldier, it is scarcely worth our while to fight against a contemptible ministry only. Dearly, dearly, do we pay for the repeal of the acts, if that is all we fight for; for in a just estimation, it is as great a folly to pay a Bunker-hill price for law, as for land. As I have always considered the independancy of this continent, as an event, which sooner or later must arrive, so from the late rapid progress of the continent to maturity, the event could not be far off. Wherefore, on the breaking out of hostilities, it was not worth the while to have disputed a matter, which time would have finally redressed, unless we meant to be in earnest; otherwise, it is like wasting an estate on a suit of law, to regulate the trespasses of a tenant, whose lease is just expiring. No man was a warmer wisher for reconciliation than myself, before the fatal nineteenth of April 1775, but the moment the event of that day was made known, I rejected the hardened, sullen tempered Pharoah of —— for ever; and disdain the wretch, that with the pretended title of FATHER OF HIS PEOPLE can unfeelingly hear of their slaughter, and composedly sleep with their blood upon his soul.

But admitting that matters were now made up, what would be the event? I answer, the ruin of the continent. And that for several reasons.

First. The powers of governing still remaining in the hands of the k——, he will have a negative over the whole legislation of this continent. And as he hath shewn himself such an inveterate enemy to liberty, and discovered such a thirst for arbitrary power; is he, or is he not, a proper man to say to these colonies, '*You shall make no laws but what I please.*' And is there any in habitants in America so ignorant, as not to know, that according to what is called the *present constitution*, that this continent can make no laws but what the king gives leave to; and is there any man so unwise, as not to see, that (considering what has happened) he will suffer no Law to be made here, but such as suit his purpose. We may be as effectually enslaved by the want of laws in America, as by submitting to laws made for us in England. After matters are made up (as it is called) can there be any doubt but the whole power of the crown will be exerted, to keep this continent as low and humble as possible? Instead of going forward we shall go backward, or be perpetually quarrelling or ridiculously petitioning. — We are already greater than the king wishes us to be, and will he not hereafter endeavour to make us less? To bring the matter to one point. Is the power who is jealous of our prosperity, a proper power to govern us? Whoever says *No* to this question is an *independent*, for independancy means no more, than, whether we shall make our own laws, or, whether the ——, the greatest enemy this continent hath, or can have, shall tell us '*there shall be no laws but such as I like.*'

But the k—— you will say has a negative in England; the people there can make no laws without his consent. In point of right and good order, there is something very ridiculous, that a youth of twenty-one (which hath often happened) shall say to several millions of people, older and wiser than himself, I forbid this or that act of yours to be law. But in this place I decline this sort of reply, tho' I will never cease to expose the absurdity of it, and only answer, that England being the kind's residence, and America not so, makes quite another case. The k——'s negative *here* is ten times more dangerous and fatal than it can be in England, for *there* he will scarcely refuse his consent to a bill for putting England into as strong a state of defence as possible, and in America he would never suffer such a bill to be passed.

America is only a secondary object in the system of British politics. England consults the good of *this* country, no farther than it answers her *own* purpose. Wherefore, her own interest leads her to suppress the growth of *ours* in every case which doth not promote her advantage, or in the least interfere with it. A pretty state we should soon be in under such a second-hand government, considering what has happened! Men do not change from enemies to friends by the alteration of a name: And in order to shew that reconciliation *now* is a dangerous doctrine, I affirm, *that it would be policy in the k——* *at this time, to repeal the acts for the sake of reinstating himself in the government of the provinces*; in order, that HE MAY ACCOMPLISH BY CRAFT AND SUBTILTY, IN THE LONG RUN, WHAT HE CAN-NOT DO BY FORCE AND VIOLENCE IN THE SHORT ONE. Reconciliation and ruin are nearly related.

Secondly, That as even the best terms, which we can expect to obtain, can amount to no more than a temporary expedient, or a kind of government by guardianship, which can last no longer than till the colonies come of age, so the general face and state of things, in the interim, will be unsettled and unpromising. Emigrants of property will not choose to come to a country whose form of government hangs but by a thread, and who is every day tottering on the brink of commotion and disturbance; and numbers of the present inhabitants would lay hold of the interval, to dispose of their effects, and quit the continent.

But the most powerful of all arguments, is, that nothing but independence, i.e. a continental form of government, can keep the peace of the continent and preserve it inviolate from civil wars. I dread the event of a reconciliation with Britain now, as it is more than probable, that it will be followed by a revolt somewhere or other, the consequences of which may be far more fatal than all the malice of Britain.

Thousands are already ruined by British barbarity; (thousands more will probably suffer the same fate.) Those men have other feelings than us who have nothing suffered. All they *now* possess is liberty, what they before enjoyed is sacrificed to its service, and having nothing more to lose, they disdain submission. Besides, the general temper of the colonies, towards a British government, will be like that of a youth, who is nearly out of his time, they will care very little about her. And a government which cannot preserve the peace, is no government at all, and in that case we pay our money for nothing; and pray what is it that Britain can do, whose power will be wholly on paper, should a civil tumult break out the very day after reconciliation? I have heard some men say, many of whom I believe spoke without thinking, that they dreaded an independence, fearing that it would produce civil wars. It is but seldom that our first thoughts are truly correct, and that is the case here; for there are ten times more to dread from a patched up connexion than from independence. I make the sufferers case my own, and I protest, that were I driven from house and home, my property destroyed, and my circumstances ruined, that as man, sensible of injuries, I could never relish the doctrine of reconciliation, or consider myself bound thereby.

The colonies have manifested such a spirit of good order and obedience to continental government, as is sufficient to make every reasonable person easy and happy on that head. No man can assign the least pretence for his fears, on any other grounds, that such as are truly childish and ridiculous, that one colony will be striving for superiority over another.

Where there are no distinctions there can be no superiority, perfect equality affords no temptation. The republics of Europe are all (and we may say always) in peace. Holland and Swisserland are without wars, foreign or domestic: Monarchical governments, it is true, are never long at rest; the crown itself is a temptation to enterprizing ruffians at *home*; and that degree of pride and insolence ever attendant on regal authority, swells into a rupture with foreign powers, in instances, where a republican government, by being formed on more natural principles, would negociate the mistake.

If there is any true cause of fear respecting independance, it is because no plan is yet laid down. Men do not see their way out — Wherefore, as an opening into that business, I offer the following hints; at the same time modestly affirming, that I have no other opinion of them myself, than that they may be the means of giving rise to something better. Could the straggling thoughts of individuals be collected, they would frequently form materials for wise and able men to improve to useful matter.

LET the assemblies be annual, with a President only. The representation more equal. Their business wholly domestic, and subject to the authority of a Continental Congress.

Let each colony be divided into six, eight, or ten, convenient districts, each district to send a proper number of delegates to Congress, so that each colony send at least thirty. The whole number in Congress will be at least 390. Each Congress to sit and to choose a president by the following method. When the delegates are met, let a colony be taken from the whole thirteen colonies by lot, after which let the whole Congress choose (by ballot) a president from out of the delegates of *that* province. In the next Congress, let a colony be taken by lot from twelve only, omitting that colony from which the president was taken in the former Congress, and so proceeding on till the whole thirteen shall have had their proper rotation. And in order that nothing may pass into a law but what is satisfactorily just, not less than three fifths of the Congress to be called a majority. — He that will promote discord, under a government so equally formed as this, would join Lucifer in his revolt.

But as there is a peculiar delicacy, from whom, or in what manner, this business must first arise, and as it seems most agreeable and consistent, that it should come from some intermediate body between the governed and the governors, that is between the Congress and the people, let a CONTINENTAL CONFERENCE be held, in the following manner, and for the following purpose.

A committee of twenty-six members of Congress, viz. two for each colony. Two members for each house of assembly, or Provincial convention; and five representatives of the people at large, to be chosen in the capital city or town of each province, for, and in behalf of the whole province, by as many qualified voters as shall think proper to attend from all parts of the province for that purpose; or, if more convenient, the representatives may be chosen in two or three of the most populous parts thereof. In this conference, thus assembled, will be united, the two grand principles of business, *knowledge* and *power*. The members of Congress, Assemblies, or Conventions, by having had experience in national concerns, will be able and useful counsellors, and the whole, being impowered by the people will have a truly legal authority.

The conferring members being met, let their business be to frame a CONTINENTAL CHARTER, or Charter of the United Colonies; (answering to what is called the Magna Charta of England) fixing the number and manner of choosing members of

Congress, members of Assembly, with their date of sitting, and drawing the line of business and jurisdiction between them: (Always
remembering, that our strength is continental, not provincial:)
Securing freedom and property to all men, and above all things the
free exercise of religion, according to the dictates of conscience; with
such other matter as is necessary for a charter to contain.
Immediately after which, the said conference to dissolve, and the
bodies which shall be chosen conformable to the said charter, to be
the legislators and governors of this continent for the time being:
Whose peace and happiness, may God preserve, Amen.

Should any body of men be hereafter delegated for this or some
similar purpose, I offer them the following extracts from that wise
observer on governments *Dragonetti*. 'The science' says he, 'of the
politician consists in fixing the true point of happiness and freedom.
Those men would deserve the gratitude of ages, who should discover
a mode of government that contained the greatest sum of individual
happiness, with the least national expence.

Dragonetti on Virtue and Rewards.'

But where says some is the King of America? I'll tell you Friend,
he reigns above, and doth not make havock of mankind like the
Royal —— of Britain. Yet that we may not appear to be defective
even in earthly honors, let a day be solemnly set apart for proclaiming the charter; let it be brought forth placed on the divine law, the
word of God; let a crown be placed thereon, by which the world may
know, that so far as we approve of monarchy, that in America THE
LAW IS KING. For as in absolute governments the King is law, so in
free countries the law *ought* to be King; and there ought to be no
other. But lest any ill use should afterwards arise, let the crown at the
conclusion of the ceremony be demolished, and scattered among the
people whose right it is.

A government of our own is our natural right: And when a man seriously reflects on the precariousness of human affairs, he will become convinced, that it is infinitely wiser and safer, to form a constitution of our own in a cool deliberate manner, while we have it in our power, than to trust such an interesting event to time and chance. If we omit it now, some Massenello may hereafter arise, who laying hold of popular disquietudes, may collect together the desperate and the discontented, and by assuming to themselves the powers of government, may sweep away the liberties of the continent like a deluge. Should the government of America return again into the hands of Britain, the tottering situation of things, will be a temptation for some desperate adventurer to try his fortune; and in such a case, what relief can Britain give? Ere she could hear the news the fatal business might be done, and ourselves suffering like the wretched Britons under the oppression of the Conqueror. Ye that oppose independance now, ye know not what ye do; ye are opening a door to eternal tyranny, by keeping vacant the seat of government. There are thousands and tens of thousands, who would think it glorious to expel from the continent, that barbarous and hellish power, which hath stirred up the Indians and Negroes to destroy us; the cruelty hath a double guilt, it is dealing brutally by us, and treacherously by them.

To talk of friendship with those in whom our reason forbids us to have faith, and our affections wounded through a thousand pores instruct us to detest, is madness and folly. Every day wears out the little remains of kindred between us and them, and can there be any reason to hope, that as the relationship expires, the affection will increase, or that we shall agree better, when we have ten times more and greater concerns to quarrel over than ever?

Ye that tell us of harmony and reconciliation, can ye restore to us the time that is past? Can ye give to prostitution its former innocence? Neither can ye reconcile Britain and America. The last cord now is broken, the people of England are presenting addresses against us. There are injuries which nature cannot forgive; she would cease to be nature if she did. As well can the lover forgive the ravisher of his mistress, as the continent forgive the murders of Britain. The Almighty hath implanted in us these unextinguishable feelings for good and wise purposes. They are the guardians of his image in our hearts. They distinguish us from the herd of common animals. The social compact would dissolve, and justice be extirpated the earth, or have only a casual existence were we callous to the touches of affection. The robber and the murderer, would often escape unpunished, did not the injuries which our tempers sustain, provoke us into justice.

O ye that love mankind! Ye that dare oppose, not only the tyranny, but the tyrant, stand forth! Every spot of the old world is over-run with oppression. Freedom hath been hunted round the globe. Asia, and Africa, have long expelled her. — Europe regards her like a stranger, and England hath given her warning to depart. O! receive the fugitive, and prepare in time an asylum for mankind.

OF THE PRESENT ABILITY OF AMERICA, WITH SOME MISELLANEOUS REFLEXIONS.

I have never met with a man, either in England or America, who hath not confessed his opinion, that a separation between the countries, would take place one time or other. And there is no instance in which we have shewn less judgment, than in endeavouring to describe, what we call, the ripeness or fitness of the Continent for independance.

As all men allow the measure, and vary only in their opinion of the time, let us, in order to remove mistakes, take a general survey of things and endeavour if possible, to find out the *very* time. But we need not go far, the inquiry ceases at once, for the *time hath found us*. The general concurrence, the glorious union of all things prove the fact.

It is not in numbers but in unity, that our great strength lies; yet our present numbers are sufficient to repel the force of all the world. The Continent hath, at this time, the largest body of armed and disciplined men of any power under Heaven; and is just arrived at that pitch of strength, in which no single colony is able to support itself, and the whole, when united can accomplish the matter, and either more, or, less than this, might be fatal in its effects. Our land force is already sufficient, and as to naval affairs, we cannot be insensible, that Britain would never suffer an American man of war to be built while the continent remained in her hands. Wherefore we should be no forwarder an hundred years hence in that branch, than we are now; but the truth is, we should be less so, because the timber of the country is every day diminishing, and that which will remain at last, will be far off and difficult to procure.

Were the continent crowded with inhabitants, her sufferings under the present circumstances would be intolerable. The more sea port towns we had, the more should we have both to defend and to loose. Our present numbers are so happily proportioned to our wants, that no man need be idle. The diminution of trade affords an army, and the necessities of an army create a new trade.

Debts we have none; and whatever we may contract on this account will serve as a glorious memento of our virtue. Can we but leave posterity with a settled form of government, an independent constitution of its own, the purchase at any price will be cheap. But to expend millions for the sake of getting a few vile acts repealed, and routing the present ministry only, is unworthy the charge, and is using posterity with the utmost cruelty; because it is leaving them the great work to do, and a debt upon their backs, from which they derive no advantage. Such a thought is unworthy a man of honor, and is the true characteristic of a narrow heart and a pedling politician.

The debt we may contract doth not deserve our regard if the work be but accomplished. No nation ought to be without a debt. A national debt is a national bond; and when it bears no interest, is in no case a grievance. Britain is oppressed with a debt of upwards of one hundred and forty millions sterling, for which she pays upwards of four millions interest. And as a compensation for her debt, she has a large navy; America is without a debt, and without a navy; yet for the twentieth part of the English national debt, could have a navy as large again. The navy of England is not worth, at this time, more than three millions and a half sterling.

The charge of building a ship of each rate, and furnishing her with masts, yards, sails and rigging, together with a proportion of eight months boatswain's and carpenter's sea-stores, as calculated by Mr Burchett, Secretary to the navy.

		£.
For a ship of 100 guns	——	35,553
90	—— ——	29,886
80	—— ——	23,638
70	—— ——	17,785
60	—— ——	14,197
50	—— ——	10,606
40	—— ——	7,558
30	—— ——	5,846
20	—— ——	3,710

And from hence it is easy to sum up the value, or cost rather, of the whole British navy, which in the year 1757, when it was at its greatest glory consisted of the following ships and guns:

Ships.	Guns.	Cost of one.	Cost of all.
6	– 100	– 35,553 l.	– 213,318 l.
12	– 90	– 29,886	– 358,632
12	– 80	– 23,638	– 283,656

43	– 70	– 17,785	– 746,755
35	– 60	– 14,197	– 496,895
40	– 50	– 10,606	– 424,240
45	– 40	– 7,558	– 340,110
58	– 20	– 3,710	– 215,180

85 Sloops, bombs,
and fireships, one ⎫ 2,000 – 170,000
with another, at ⎭

                Cost 3,266,786
Remains for guns, —   233,214

           Total, 3,500,000

No country on the globe is so happily situated, or so internally capable of raising a fleet as America. Tar, timber, iron, and cordage are her natural produce. We need go abroad for nothing. Whereas the Dutch, who make large profits by hiring out their ships of war to the Spaniards and Portuguese, are obliged to import most of the materials they use. We ought to view the building a fleet as an article of commerce, it being the natural manufactory of this country. It is the best money we can lay out. A navy when finished is worth more than it cost. And is that nice point in national policy, in which commerce and protection are united. Let us build; if we want them not, we can sell; and by that means replace our paper currency with ready gold and silver.

In point of manning a fleet, people in general run into great errors; it is not necessary that one-fourth part should be sailors. The Terrible privateer, Captain Death, stood the hottest engagement of any ship last war, yet had not twenty sailors on board, though her complement of men was upwards of two hundred. A few able and social sailors will soon instruct a sufficient number of active land-men in the common work of a ship. Wherefore, we never can be more capable to begin on maritime matters than now, while our timber is standing, our fisheries blocked up, and our sailors and shipwrights out of employ. Men of war of seventy and 80 guns were built forty years ago in New-England, and why not the same now? Ship-building is America's greatest pride, and in which, she will in time excel the whole world. The great empires of the east are mostly inland, and consequently excluded from the possibility of rivalling her. Africa is in a state of barbarism; and no power in Europe, hath either such an extent or coast, or such an internal supply of materials. Where nature hath given the one, she has withheld the other; to America only hath she been liberal of both. The vast empire of Russia is almost shut out from the sea; wherefore, her boundless forests, her tar, iron, and cordage are only articles of commerce.

In point of safety, ought we to be without a fleet? We are not the little people now, which we were sixty years ago; at that time we might have trusted our property in the streets, or fields rather; and slept securely without locks or bolts to our doors or windows. The case now is altered, and our methods of defence ought to improve with our increase of property. A common pirate, twelve months ago, might have come up the Delaware, and laid the city of Philadelphia under instant contribution, for what sum he pleased; and the same might have happened to other places. Nay, any daring fellow, in a brig of fourteen or sixteen guns, might have robbed the whole Continent, and carried off half a million of money. These are circumstances which demand our attention, and point out the necessity of naval protection.

Some, perhaps, will say, that after we have made it up with Britain, she will protect us. Can they be so unwise as to mean, that she shall keep a navy in our harbours for that purpose? Common sense will tell us, that the power which hath endeavoured to subdue us, is of all others the most improper to defend us. Conquest may be effected under the pretence of friendship; and ourselves, after a long and brave resistance, be at last cheated into slavery. And if her ships are not to be admitted into our harbours, I would ask, how is she to protect us? A navy three or four thousand miles off can be of little use, and on sudden emergencies, none at all. Wherefore, if we must hereafter protect ourselves, why not do it for ourselves? Why do it for another?

The English list of ships of war is long and formidable, but not a tenth part of them are at any one time fit for service, numbers of them are not in being; yet their names are pompously continued in the list; if only a plank be left of the ship: and not a fifth part, of such as are fit for service, can be spared on any one station at one time. The East, and West Indies, Mediterranean, Africa, and other parts over which Britain extends her claim, make large demands upon her navy. From a mixture of prejudice and inattention, we have contracted a false notion respecting the navy of England, and have talked as if we should have the whole of it to encounter at once, and for that reason, supposed that we must have one as large; which not being instantly practicable, have been made use of by a set of disguised Tories to discourage our beginning thereon. Nothing can be farther from truth than this; for if America had only a twentieth part of the naval force of Britain, she would be by far an over match for her; because, as we neither have, nor claim any foreign dominion, our whole force would be employed on our own coast, where we should, in the long run, have two to one the advantage of those who had three or four thousand miles to sail over, before they could attack us, and the same distance to return in order to refit and recruit. And although Britain by her fleet, hath a check over our trade to Europe, we have as large a one over her trade to the West-Indies, which, by laying in the neighbourhood of the Continent, is entirely at its mercy.

Some method might be fallen on to keep up a naval force in time of peace, if we should not judge it necessary to support a constant navy. If premiums were to be given to merchants, to build and employ in their service, ships mounted with twenty, thirty, forty, or fifty guns, (the premiums to be in proportion to the loss of bulk to the merchants) fifty or sixty of those ships, with a few guard ships on constant duty, would keep up a sufficient navy, and that without burdening ourselves with the evil so loudly complained of in England, of suffering their fleet, in time of peace to lie rotting in the docks. To unite the sinews of commerce and defence is sound policy; for when our strength and our riches play into each other's hand, we need fear no external enemy.

In almost every article of defence we abound. Hemp flourishes even to rankness, so that we need not want cordage. Our iron is superior to that of other countries. Our small arms equal to any in the world. Cannon we can cast at pleasure. Saltpetre and gunpowder we are every day producing. Our knowledge is hourly improving. Resolution is our inherent character, and courage hath never yet forsaken us. Wherefore, what is it that we want? Why is it that we hesitate? From Britain we can expect nothing but ruin. If she is once admitted to the government of America again, this Continent will not be worth living in. Jealousies will be always arising; insurrections will be constantly happening; and who will go forth to quell them? Who will venture his life to reduce his own countrymen to a foreign obedience? The difference between Pennsylvania and Connecticut, respecting some unlocated lands, shews the insignificance of a B——sh government, and fully proves, that nothing but Continental authority can regulate Continental matters.

Another reason why the present time is preferable to all others, is, that the fewer our numbers are, the more land there is yet unoccupied, which instead of being lavished by the k—— on his worthless dependents, may be hereafter applied, not only to the discharge of the present debt, but to the constant support of government. No nation under Heaven hath such an advantage as this.

The infant state of the Colonies, as it is called, so far from being against, is an argument in favor of independance. We are sufficiently numerous, and were we more so, we might be less united. It is a matter worthy of observation, that the more a country is peopled, the smaller their armies are. In military numbers, the ancients far exceeded the moderns: and the reason is evident, for trade being the consequence of population, men become too much absorbed thereby to attend to any thing else. Commerce diminishes the spirit, both of patriotism and military defence. And history sufficiently informs us, that the bravest achievements were always accomplished in the nonage of a nation. With the increase of commerce, England hath lost its spirit. The city of London, notwithstanding its numbers, submits to continued insults with the patience of a coward. The more men have to lose, the less willing are they to venture. The rich are in general slaves to fear, and submit to courtly power with the trembling duplicity of a spaniel.

Youth is the seed time of good habits, as well in nations as in individuals. It might be difficult, if not impossible, to form the Continent into one government half a century hence. The vast variety of interests, occasioned by an increase of trade and population, would create confusion. Colony would be against colony. Each being able might scorn each other's assistance: and while the proud and foolish gloried in their little distinctions, the wise would lament that the union had not been formed before. Wherefore, the *present time is the true time* for establishing it. The intimacy which is contracted in infancy, and the friendship which is formed in misfortune, are, of all others, the most lasting and unalterable. Our present union is marked with both these characters: we are young, and we have been distressed; but our concord hath withstood our troubles, and fixes a memorable æra for posterity to glory in.

The present time, likewise, is that peculiar time, which never happens to a nation but once, *viz.* the time of forming itself into a government. Most nations have let slip the opportunity, and by that means have been compelled to receive laws from their conquerors, instead of making laws for themselves. First, they had a king, and then a form of government; whereas the articles or charter of government should be formed first, and men delegated to execute them afterward: but from the errors of other nations, let us learn wisdom, and lay hold of the present opportunity — *To begin government at the right end.*

When William the conqueror subdued England he gave them law at the point of the sword; and until we consent that the seat of government in America, be legally and authoritatively occupied, we shall be in danger of having it filled by some fortunate ruffian, who may treat us in the same manner, and then, where will be our freedom? where our property?

As to religion, I hold it to be the indispensible duty of all government, to protect all conscientious professors thereof, and I know of no other business which government hath to do therewith. Let a man throw aside that narrowness of soul, that selfishness of principle, which the niggards of all professions are so unwilling to part with, and he will be at once delivered of his fears on that head. Suspicion is the companion of mean souls, and the bane of all good society. For myself I fully and conscientiously believe, that it is the will of the Almighty, that there should be a diversity of religious opinions among us: It affords a larger field for our christian kindness. Were we all of one way of thinking, our religious dispositions would want matter for probation; and on this liberal principle, I look on the various denominations among us, to be like children of the same family, differing only, in what is called their Christian names.

In page fifty-four,* I threw out a few thoughts on the propriety of a Continental Charter, (for I only presume to offer hints, not plans) and in this place, I take the liberty of rementioning the subject, by observing, that a charter is to be understood as a bond of

* [Page 181 in this edition.]

solemn obligation, which the whole enters into, to support the right of every separate part, whether of religion, personal freedom, or property. A firm bargain and a right reckoning make long friends.

In a former page I likewise mentioned the necessity of a large and equal representation; and there is no political matter which more deserves our attention. A small number of electors, or a small number of representatives, are equally dangerous. But if the number of the representatives be not only small, but unequal, the danger is increased. As an instance of this, I mention the following; when the Associators petition was before the House of Assembly of Pennsylvania; twenty-eight members only were present, all the Bucks county members, being eight, voted against it, and had seven of the Chester members done the same, this whole province had been governed by two counties only, and this danger it is always exposed to. The unwarrantable stretch likewise, which that house made in their last sitting, to gain an undue authority over the Delegates of that province, ought to warn the people at large, how they trust power out of their own hands. A set of instructions for the Delegates were put together, which in point of sense and business would have dis-honored a school-boy, and after being approved by a *few*, a *very few* without doors, were carried into the House, and there passed *in behalf of the whole colony*; whereas, did the whole colony know, with what ill-will that House hath entered on some necessary public measures, they would not hesitate a moment to think them unworthy of such a trust.

Immediate necessity makes many things convenient, which if continued would grow into oppressions. Expedience and right are different things. When the calamities of America required a consultation, there was no method so ready, or at that time so proper, as to appoint persons from the several Houses of Assembly for that purpose and the wisdom with which they have proceeded hath preserved this continent from ruin. But as it is more than probable that we shall never be without a CONGRESS, every well wisher to good order, must own, that the mode for choosing members of that body, deserves consideration. And I put it as a question to those, who make a study of mankind, whether *representation and election* is not too great a power for one and the same body of men to possess? When we are planning for posterity, we ought to remember that virtue is not hereditary.

It is from our enemies that we often gain excellent maxims, and are frequently surprised into reason by their mistakes. Mr Cornwall (one of the Lords of the Treasury) treated the petition of the New-York Assembly with contempt, because *that* House, he said, consisted but of twenty-six members, which trifling number, he argued, could not with decency be put for the whole. We thank him for his involuntary honesty.

TO CONCLUDE, however strange it may appear to some, or however unwilling they may be to think so, matters not, but many strong and striking reasons may be given, to shew, that nothing can settle our affairs so expeditiously as an open and determined declaration for independance. Some of which are,

First. — It is the custom of nations, when any two are at war, for some other powers, not engaged in the quarrel, to step in as mediators, and bring about the preliminaries of a peace: but while America calls herself the subject of Great Britain, no power, however well disposed she may be, can offer her mediation. Wherefore, in our present state we may quarrel on for ever.

Secondly. — It is unreasonable to suppose, that France or Spain will give us any kind of assistance, if we mean only to make use of that assistance for the purpose of repairing the breach, and strengthening the connection between Britain and America; because, those powers would be sufferers by the consequences.

Thirdly. — While we profess ourselves the subjects of Britain, we must, in the eye of foreign nations, be considered as rebels. The precedent is somewhat dangerous to *their peace*, for men to be in arms under the name of subjects; we on the spot, can solve the paradox: but to unite resistance and subjection, requires an idea much too refined for common understanding.

Fourthly. — Were a manifesto to be published, and despatched to foreign courts, setting forth the miseries we have endured, and the peaceable methods we have ineffectually used for redress; declaring, at the same time, that not being able, any longer to live happily or safely under the cruel disposition of the B——sh court, we had been driven to the necessity of breaking off all connection with her; at the same time assuring all such courts of our peaceable disposition towards them, and of our desire of entering into trade with them: Such a memorial would produce more good effects to this Continent, than if a ship were freighted with petitions to Britain.

Under our present denomination of British subjects we can neither be received nor heard abroad: The custom of all courts is against us, and will be so, until, by an independance, we take rank with other nations.

These proceedings may at first seem strange and difficult; but, like all other steps which we have already passed over, will in a little time become familiar and agreeable; and, until an independance is declared, the Continent will feel itself like a man who continues putting off some unpleasant business from day to day, yet knows it must be done, hates to set about it, wishes it over, and is continually haunted with the thoughts of its necessity.

APPENDIX

SINCE the publication of the first edition of this pamphlet, or rather, on the same day on which it came out, the ——'s Speech made its appearance in this city. Had the spirit of prophecy directed the birth of this production, it could not have brought it forth, at a more seasonable juncture, or at a more necessary time. The bloody mindedness of the one, shew the necessity of pursuing the doctrine of the other. Men read by way of revenge. And the speech instead of terrifying, prepared a way for the manly principles of Independance.

Ceremony, and even, silence, from whatever motive they may arise, have a hurtful tendency, when they give the least degree of countenance to base and wicked performances; wherefore, if this maxim be admitted, it naturally follows, that the ——'s speech, as being a piece of finished villainy, deserved, and still deserves, a general execration both by the Congress and the people. Yet as the domestic tranquillity of a nation, depends greatly on the *chastity* of what might properly be called NATIONAL MATTERS, it is often better to pass some things over in silent disdain, than to make use of such new methods of dislike, as might introduce the least innovation, on that guardian of our peace and safety. And perhaps, it is chiefly owing to this prudent delicacy, that the ——'s Speech, hath not before now, suffered a public execution. The Speech if it may be called one, is nothing better than a wilful audacious libel against the truth, the common good, and the existence of mankind; and is a formal and pompous method of offering up human sacrifices to the pride of tyrants. But this general massacre of mankind, is one of the privileges, and the certain consequences of K——s; for as nature knows them *not*, they know *not her*, and although they are beings of our *own* creating, they know not *us*, and are become the gods of their creators. The speech hath one good quality, which is, that it is not calculated to deceive, neither can we, even if we would, be deceived by it. Brutality and tyranny appear on the face of it. It leaves us at no loss: And every line convinces, even in the moment of reading, that He, who hunts the woods for prey, the naked and untutored Indian, is less a Savage than the —— of B——.

Sir J——n D——e, the putative father of a whining jesuitical piece, fallaciously called, 'The Address of the people of ENGLAND to the inhabitants of AMERICA,' hath, perhaps from a vain supposition,

that the people *here* were to be frightened at the pomp and description of a king, given, (though very unwisely on his part) the real
character of the present one: 'But,' says this writer, 'if you are
inclined to pay compliments to an administration, which we do not
complain of,' (meaning the Marquis of Rockingham's at the repeal of
the Stamp Act) 'it is very unfair in you to withhold them from that
prince, *by whose* NOD ALONE *they were permitted to do any thing.*' this
is toryism with a witness! Here is idolatry even without a mask: And
he who can calmly hear, and digest such doctrine, hath forfeited his
claim to rationality — an apostate from the order of manhood; and
ought to be considered — as one, who hath, not only given up the
proper dignity of a man, but sunk himself beneath the rank of animals, and contemptibly crawl through the world like a worm.

However, it matters very little now, what the —— of E——
either says or does; he hath wickedly broken through every moral
and human obligation, trampled nature and conscience beneath his
feet; and by a steady and constitutional spirit of insolence and cruelty, procured for himself an universal hatred. It is *now* the interest
of America to provide for herself. She hath already a large and young
family, whom it is more her duty to take care of, than to be granting
away her property, to support a power who is become a reproach to
the names of men and christians — YE, whose office it is to watch
over the morals of a nation, of whatsoever sect or denomination ye
are of, as well as ye, who are more immediately the guardians of the
public liberty, if ye wish to preserve your native country uncontami-
nated by European corruption, ye must in secret wish a separation —
But leaving the moral part to private reflection, I shall chiefly con-
fine my farther remarks to the following heads.

First, That it is the interest of America to be separated from
Britain.

Secondly. Which is the easiest and most practicable plan, REC-
ONCILIATION or INDEPENDANCE? with some occasional remarks.

In support of the first, I could, if I judged it proper, produce the opinion of some of the ablest and most experienced men on this continent; and whose sentiments, on that head, are not yet publickly known. It is in reality a self-evident position: For no nation in a state of foreign dependance, limited in its commerce, and cramped and fettered in its legislative powers, can ever arrive at any material eminence. America doth not yet know what opulence is; and although the progress which she hath made stands unparalleled in the history of other nations, it is but childhood, compared with what she would be capable of arriving at, had she, as she ought to have, the legislative powers in her own hands. England is, at this time, proudly coveting what would do her no good, were she to accomplish it; and the Continent hesitating on a matter, which will be her final ruin if neglected. It is the commerce and not the conquest of America, by which England is to be benefited, and that would in a great measure continue, were the countries as independant of each other as France and Spain; because in many articles, neither can go to a better market. But it is the independance of this country on Britain or any other, which is now the main and only object worthy of contention, and which, like all other truths discovered by necessity, will appear clearer and stronger every day.

First. Because it will come to that one time or other.

Secondly. Because the longer it is delayed the harder it will be to accomplish.

I have frequently amused myself both in public and private companies, with silently remarking the spacious errors of those who speak without reflecting. And among the many which I have heard, the following seems the most general, viz. that had this rupture happened forty or fifty years hence, instead of *now*, the Continent would have been more able to have shaken off the dependance. To which I reply, that our military ability *at this time*, arises from the experience gained in the last war, and which in forty or fifty years time, would have been totally extinct. The Continent, would not, by that time, have had a General, or even a military officer left; and we, or those who may succeed us, would have been as ignorant of martial matters as the ancient Indians: And this single position, closely attended to, will unanswerably prove, that the present time is preferable to all others: The argument turns thus — at the conclusion of the last war, we had experience, but wanted numbers; and forty or fifty years hence, we should have numbers, without experience; wherefore, the proper point of time, must be some particular point between the two extremes, in which a sufficiency of the former remains, and a proper increase of the latter is obtained: And that point of time is the present time.

The reader will pardon this digression, as it does not properly come under the head I first set out with, and to which I again return by the following position, viz.

Should affairs be patched up with Britain, and she to remain the governing and sovereign power of America, (which as matters are now circumstanced, is giving up the point entirely) we shall deprive ourselves of the very means of sinking the debt we have or may contract. The value of the back lands which some of the provinces are clandestinely deprived of, by the unjust extension of the limits of Canada, valued only at five pounds sterling per hundred acres, amount to upwards of twenty-five millions, Pennsylvania currency; and the quit-rents at one penny sterling per acre, to two millions yearly.

It is by the sale of those lands that the debt may be sunk, without burthen to any, and the quit-rent reserved thereon, will always lessen, and in time will wholly support the yearly expence of government. It matters not how long the debt is in paying, so that the lands when sold be applied to the discharge of it, and for the execution of which, the Congress for the time being, will be the continental trustees.

I proceed now to the second head, viz. Which is the earliest and most practicable plan, RECONCILIATION or INDEPENDANCE? with some occasional remarks.

He who takes nature for his guide, is not easily beaten out of his argument, and on that ground, I answer *generally — That* INDEPEN-DANCE *being a* SINGLE SIMPLE LINE, *contained within ourselves; and reconciliation, a matter exceedingly perplexed and complicated, and in which, a treacherous capricious court is to interfere, gives the answer without a doubt.*

The present state of America is truly alarming to every man who is capable of reflection. Without law, without government, without any other mode of power than what is founded on, and granted by courtesy. Held together by an unexampled concurrence of sentiment, which is nevertheless subject to change, and which every secret enemy is endeavouring to dissolve. Our present condition, is, Legislation without law; wisdom without a plan; a constitution without a name; and, what is strangely astonishing, perfect Independance contending for Dependance. The instance is without a precedent; the case never existed before; and who can tell what may be the event? The property of no man is secure in the present unbraced system of things. The mind of the multitude is left at random, and feeling no fixed object before them, they pursue such as fancy or opinion starts. Nothing is criminal; there is no such thing as treason; wherefore, every one thinks himself at liberty to act as he pleases. The Tories dared not to have assembled offensively, had they known that their lives, by that act were forfeited to the laws of the state. A line of distinction should be drawn, between English soldiers taken in battle, and inhabitants of America taken in arms. The first are prisoners, but the latter traitors. The one forfeits his liberty the other his head.

Notwithstanding our wisdom, there is a visible feebleness in some of our proceedings which gives encouragement to dissentions.

The Continental belt is too loosely buckled. And if something is not done in time, it will be too late to do any thing, and we shall fall into a state, in which, neither *reconciliation* nor *independance* will be practicable. The —— and his worthless adherents are got at their old game of dividing the Continent, and there are not wanting among us, Printers, who will be busy in spreading specious falsehoods. The artful and hypocritical letter which appeared a few months ago in two of the New-York papers, and likewise in two others, is an evidence that there are men who want either judgement or honesty.

It is easy getting into holes and corners and talking of reconciliation: But do such men seriously consider, how difficult the task is, and how dangerous it may prove, should the Continent divide thereon. Do they take within their view, all the various orders of men whose situation and circumstances, as well as their own, are to be considered therein. Do they put themselves in the place of the sufferer whose *all* is *already* gone, and of the soldier, who hath quitted *all* for the defence of his country. If their ill-judged moderation be suited to their own private situations *only*, regardless of others, the event will convince them, that 'they are reckoning without their Host.'

Put us, says some, on the footing we were on in sixty-three: To which I answer, the request is not *now* in the power of Britain to comply with, neither will she propose it; but if it were, and even should be granted, I ask, as a reasonable question, By what means is such a corrupt and faithless court to be kept to its engagements? Another parliament, nay, even the present, may hereafter repeal the obligation, on the pretence of its being violently obtained, or unwisely granted; and in that case, Where is our redress? — No going to law with nations; cannon are the barristers of crowns; and the sword, not of justice, but of war, decides the suit. To be on the footing of sixty-three, it is not sufficient, that the laws only be put on the same state, but, that our circumstances, likewise be put on the same state; our burnt and destroyed towns repaired or built up, our private losses made good, our public debts (contracted for defence) discharged; otherwise, we shall be millions worse than we were at that enviable period. Such a request had it been complied with a year ago, would have won the heart and soul of the Continent — but now it is too late, 'The Rubicon is passed.'

Besides the taking up arms, merely to enforce the repeal of a pecuniary law, seems as unwarrantable by the divine law, and as repugnant to human feelings, as the taking up arms to enforce obedience thereto. The object, on either side, doth not justify the ways and means; for the lives of men are too valuable to be cast away on such trifles. It is the violence which is done and threatened to our persons; the destruction of our property by an armed force; the invasion of our country by fire and sword, which conscientiously qualifies the use of arms: And the instant, in which such mode of defence became necessary, all subjection to Britain ought to have ceased; and the independancy of America should have been considered, as dating its æra from, and published by, *the first musket that was fired against her.* This line is a line of consistency; neither drawn by caprice, nor extended by ambition; but produced by a chain of events, of which the colonies were not the authors.

I shall conclude these remarks, with the following timely and well intended hints. We ought to reflect, that there are three different ways by which an independancy may hereafter be effected; and that *one* of those *three*, will one day or other, be the fate of America, viz. By the legal voice of the people in Congress; by a military power; or by a mob: It may not always happen that our soldiers are citizens, and the multitude a body of reasonable men; virtue, as I have already remarked, is not hereditary, neither is it perpetual. Should an independancy be brought about by the first of those means, we have every opportunity and every encouragement before us, to form the noblest, purest constitution on the face of the earth. We have it in our power to begin the world over again. A situation, similar to the present, hath not happened since the days of Noah until now. The birth-day of a new world is at hand, and a race of men perhaps as numerous as all Europe contains, are to receive their portion of freedom from the event of a few months. The Reflexion is awful — and in this point of view, How trifling, how ridiculous, do the little, paltry cavellings, of a few weak or interested men appear, when weighed against the business of a world.

Should we neglect the present favorable and inviting period, and an independance be hereafter effected by any other means, we must charge the consequence to ourselves, or to those rather, whose narrow and prejudiced souls, are habitually opposing the measure, without either inquiring or reflecting. There are reasons to be given in support of Independance, which men should rather privately think of, than be publicly told of. We ought not now to be debating whether we shall be independant or not, but, anxious to accomplish it on a firm, secure, and honorable basis, and uneasy rather that it is not yet began upon. Every day convinces us of its necessity. Even the Tories (if such beings yet remain among us) should, of all men, be the most solicitous to promote it; for, as the appointment of committees at first, protected them from popular rage, so, a wise and well established form of government, will be the only certain means of continuing it securely to them. *Wherefore*, if they have not virtue enough to be WHIGS, they ought to have prudence enough to wish for Independance.

In short, Independance is the only BOND that tye and keep us together. We shall then see our object, and our ears will be legally shut against the schemes of an intriguing, as well as cruel enemy. We shall then too, be on a proper footing, to treat with Britain; for there is reason to conclude, that the pride of that court, will be less hurt by treating with the American states for terms of peace, than with those, whom she denominates, 'rebellious subjects,' for terms of accommodation. It is our delaying it that encourages her to hope for conquest, and our backwardness tends only to prolong the war. As we have, without any good effect therefrom, with-held our trade to obtain a redress of our grievances, let us *now* try the alternative, by *independantly* redressing them ourselves, and then offering to open the trade. The mercantile and reasonable part of England will be still with us; because, peace, *with* trade, is preferable to war *without* it. And if this offer be not accepted, other courts may be applied to.

On these grounds I rest the matter. And as no offer hath yet been made to refute the doctrine contained in the former editions of this pamphlet, it is a negative proof, that either the doctrine cannot be refuted, or, that the party in favor of it are too numerous to be opposed. Wherefore, instead of gazing at each other with suspicious or doubtful curiosity, let each of us, hold out to his neighbor the hearty hand of friendship, and unite in drawing a line, which, like an act of oblivion, shall bury in forgetfulness every former dissention. Let the names of Whig and Tory be extinct; and let none other be heard among us, than those of *a good citizen, an open and resolute friend, and a virtuous supporter of the* rights *of* mankind, *and of the* free and independant states of america.

*

To the Representatives of the Religious Society of the People called Quakers, or to so many of them as were concerned in publishing a late piece, entitled 'The Ancient Testimony and Principles of the people called Quakers renewed, with respect to the King and Government, and Touching the Commotions now prevailing in these and other parts of America, addressed to the people in general.'

THE Writer of this, is one of those few, who never dishonors religion either by ridiculing, or cavilling at any denomination whatsoever. To God, and not to man, are all men accountable on the score of religion. Wherefore, this epistle is not so properly addressed to you as a religious, but as a political body, dabbling in matters, which the professed Quietude of your Principles instruct you not to meddle with.

As you have, without a proper authority for so doing, put yourselves in the place of the whole body of the Quakers, so, the writer of this, in order to be on an equal rank with yourselves, is under the necessity, of putting himself in the place of all those who approve the very writings and principles, against which your testimony is directed: And he hath chosen their singular situation, in order that you might discover in him, that presumption of character which you cannot see in yourselves. For neither he nor you have any claim or title to *Political Representation*.

When men have departed from the right way, it is no wonder that they stumble and fall. And it is evident from the manner in which ye have managed your testimony, that politics, (as a religious body of men) is not your proper Walk; for however well adapted it might appear to you, it is, nevertheless, a jumble of good and bad put unwisely together, and the conclusion drawn therefrom, both unnatural and unjust.

The two first pages, (and the whole doth not make four) we give you credit for, and expect the same civility from you, because the love and desire of peace is not confined to Quakerism, it is the *natural*, as well as the religious wish of all denominations of men. And on this ground, as men labouring to establish an Independant Constitution of our own, do we exceed all others in our hope, end, and aim. *Our plan is peace for ever.* We are tired of contention with Britain, and can see no real end to it but in a final separation. We act consistently, because for the sake of introducing an endless an uninterrupted peace, do we bear the evils and burthens of the present day.

We are endeavouring, and will steadily continue to endeavor, to separate and dissolve a connexion which hath already filled our land with blood; and which, while the name of it remains, will be the fatal cause of future mischiefs to both countries.

We fight neither for revenge nor conquest; neither from pride nor passion; we are not insulting the world with our fleets and armies, nor ravaging the globe for plunder. Beneath the shade of our own vines are we attacked; in our own houses, and on our own lands, is the violence committed against us. We view our enemies in the characters of Highwaymen and Housebreakers, and having no defence for ourselves in the civil law, are obliged to punish them by the military one, and apply the sword, in the very case, where you have before now, applied the halter. — Perhaps we feel for the ruined and insulted sufferers in all and every part of the continent, and with a degree of tenderness which hath not yet made its way into some of your bosoms. But be ye sure that ye mistake not the cause and ground of your Testimony. Call not coldness of soul, religion; nor put the *Bigot* in the place of the *Christian*.

O ye partial ministers of your own acknowledged principles. If the bearing arms be sinful, the first going to war must be more so, by all the difference between wilful attack and unavoidable defence. Wherefore, if ye really preach from conscience, and mean not to make a political hobby-horse of your religion, convince the world thereof, by proclaiming your doctrine to our enemies, *for they likewise bear* ARMS. Give us proof of your sincerity by publishing it at St. James's, to the commanders in chief at Boston, to the Admirals and Captains who are piratically ravaging our coasts, and to all the murdering miscreants who are acting in authority under HIM whom ye profess to serve. Had ye the honest soul of *Barclay* ye would preach repentance to *your* king; Ye would tell the Royal — his sins, and warn him of eternal ruin. Ye would not spend your partial invectives against the injured and the insulted only, but like faithful ministers, would cry aloud and *spare none*. Say not that ye are persecuted, neither endeav-our to make us the authors of that reproach, which, ye are bringing upon yourselves; for we testify unto all men, that we do not complain against you because ye are *Quakers*, but because ye pretend to *be* and are NOT Quakers.

Alas! It seems by the particular tendency of some part of your testimony, and other parts of your conduct, as if all sin was reduced to, and comprehended in *the act of bearing arms*, and that by the *peo-ple only*. Ye appear to us, to have mistaken party for conscience, because the general tenor of your actions wants unifomity: And it is exceedingly difficult to us to give credit to many of your pretended scruples; because we see them made by the same men, who, in the very instant that they are exclaiming against the mammon of this world, are nevertheless, hunting after it with a step as steady as Time, and an appetite as keen as Death.

The quotation which ye have made from Proverbs, in the third page of your testimony, that, 'when a man's ways please the Lord, he maketh even his enemies to be at peace with him'; is very unwisely chosen on your part; because it amounts to a proof, that the king's ways (whom ye are so desirous of supporting) do *not* please the Lord, otherwise, his reign would be in peace.

I now proceed to the latter part of your testimony, and that, for which all the foregoing seems only an introduction, viz.

'It hath ever been our judgment and principle, since we were called to profess the light of Christ Jesus, manifested in our con-sciences unto this day, that the setting up and putting down kings and governments, is God's peculiar prerogative; for causes best known to himself: And that it is not our business to have any hand or contrivance therein; nor to be busy bodies above our station, much less to plot and contrive the ruin, or overturn any of them, but to pray for the king, and safety of our nation, and good of all men: That we may live a peaceable and quiet life, in all goodliness and honesty; *under the government which God is pleased to set over us.'* — If these are *really* your principles why do ye not abide by them? Why do ye not leave that, which ye call God's Work, to be managed by himself? These very principles instruct you to wait with patience and humility, for the event of all public measures, and to receive *that event* as the divine will towards you. *Wherefore,* what occasion is there for your *political testimony* if you fully believe what it contains? And the very publishing it proves, that either, ye do not believe what ye profess, or have not virtue enough to practise what ye believe.

The principles of Quakerism have a direct tendency to make a man the quiet and inoffensive subject of any, and every government *which is set over him.* And if the setting up and putting down of kings and governments is God's peculiar prerogative, he most certainly will not be robbed thereof by us; wherefore, the principle itself leads you to approve of every thing, which ever happened, or may happen to kings as being his work, Oliver Cromwell thanks you. — Charles, then, died not by the hands of man; and should the present Proud Imitator of him, come to the same untimely end, the writers and publishers of the testimony, are bound by the doctrine it contains, to applaud the fact. Kings are not taken away by miracles, neither are changes in governments brought about by any other means than such as are common and human; and such as we are now using. Even the dispersing of the Jews, though foretold by our Saviour, was effected by arms. Wherefore, as ye refuse to be the means on one side, ye ought not to be meddlers on the other; but to wait the issue in silence; and unless you can produce divine authority, to prove, that the Almighty who hath created and placed this *new* world, at the greatest distance it could possibly stand, east and west, from every part of the old, doth, nevertheless, disapprove of its being independant of the corrupt and abandoned court of B——n, unless I say, ye can show this, how can ye, on the ground of your principles, justify the exciting and stirring up of the people 'firmly to unite in the *abhorrence* of all such *writings*, and *measures*, as evidence a desire and design to break off the *happy* connexion we have hitherto enjoyed, with the kingdom of Great-Britain, and our just and necessary subordination to the king, and those who are lawfully placed in authority under him.' What a slap in the face is here! the men, who, in the very paragraph before, have quietly and passively resigned up the ordering, altering, and disposal of kings and governments, into the hands of God, are now recalling their principles, and putting in for a share of the business. Is it possible, that the conclusion, which is here justly quoted, can any ways follow from the doctrine laid down? The inconsistency is too glaring not to be seen; the absurdity too great not to be laughed at; and such as could only have been made by those, whose understandings were darkened by the narrow and crabby spirit of a despairing political party; for ye are not to be considered as the whole body of the Quakers but only as a factional and fractional part thereof.

Here ends the examination of your testimony; (which I call upon no man to abhor, as ye have done, but only to read and judge of fairly;) to which I subjoin the following remark; 'That the setting up and putting down of kings,' most certainly mean, the making him a king, who is yet not so, and the making him no king who is already one. And pray what hath this to do in the present case? We neither mean to *set up* nor to *put down*, neither to *make* nor to *unmake*, but to have nothing to *do* with them. Wherefore, your testimony in whatever light it is viewed serves only to dishonour your judgment, and for many other reasons had better have been let alone than published.

First. Because it tends to the decrease and reproach of all religion whatever, and is of the utmost danger to society, to make it a party in political disputes.

Secondly. Because it exhibits a body of men, numbers of whom disavow the publishing political testimonies, as being concerned therein and approvers thereof.

Thirdly. Because it hath a tendency to undo that continental harmony and friendship which yourselves by your late liberal and charitable donations hath lent a hand to establish; and the preservation of which, is of the utmost consequence to us all.

And here without anger or resentment I bid you farewell. Sincerely wishing, that as men and christians, ye may always fully and uninterruptedly enjoy every civil and religious right; and be, in your turn, the means of securing it to others; but that the example which ye have unwisely set, of mingling religion with politics, *may be disavowed and reprabated by every inhabitant of* AMERICA.

FINIS

NOTES

1: A DECLARATION OF DEPENDENCE

. . . we most devoutly . . . Declaration of the Causes and Necessity
of Taking up Arms

That these united . . . The Declaration of Independence

Ancient prejudices . . . Thomas Paine, "Common Sense," in *Thomas
Paine: Collected Writings*, ed. Eric Foner, (New York: Library
of America, 1995), 22

Paltry rascally origin . . . Ibid., 17

French bastard . . . Ibid., 17

How a race of men . . . Ibid., 12

Whether they are . . . Ibid., 12

Wounds of deadly . . . Ibid., 27

An expression of . . . Thomas Jefferson to Henry Lee, May 8, 1825,
in *Thomas Jefferson: Writings*, ed. Merrill D. Peterson, (New
York: Library of America, 1984), 1501

2: ". . . AN ENGLISHMAN"

It is worth . . . Eric Foner, *Tom Paine and Revolutionary America*,
(London: Oxford University Press, 1976), 4

The county of Yorkshire . . . Thomas Paine, "The Rights of Man Part
I," in *Thomas Paine: Collected Writings*, ed. Eric Foner, 470

I happened . . . Thomas Paine, "The American Crisis III," in *Thomas
Paine: Collected Writings*, ed. Eric Foner, 132

The natural bent of . . . Thomas Paine, "The Age of Reason I," in
    Thomas Paine: Collected Writings, ed. Eric Foner, 701

Barren study of . . . Ibid., 697

A tolerable stock of . . . Ibid., 701

Little more than 16 . . . Thomas Paine, "The Rights of Man Part II,"
    in *Thomas Paine: Collected Writings*, ed. Eric Foner, 604

The affectionate and good . . . Jack Fruchtman Jr., *Thomas Paine:
    Apostle of Freedom*, (New York: Four Walls Eight Windows,
    1994), 23; Thomas Paine, "The Rights of Man Part II," in
    Thomas Paine: Collected Writings, ed. Eric Foner, 605

In spite of . . . Fruchtman, 24–25

The channels of trade . . . Fruchtman, 25; Thomas Paine, "The
    Rights of Man Part II," in *Thomas Paine: Collected Writings*,
    ed. Foner, 600

In what would become . . . David Freeman Hawke, *Paine*, (New York:
    W.W. Norton & Company, 1974), 11

It was levied . . . Fruchtman, 27

Nor was it lucrative . . . Ibid., 27, 28

Victualler's stocks . . . Ibid., 28

The salary of a . . . Hawke, *Paine*, 13

His appeal was granted . . . Hawke, *Paine*, 12–14; Foner, *Tom Paine
    and Revolutionary America*, 2–3; Fruchtman, 28–30

In what seems . . . Fruchtman, 31

Many friends, rich and . . . Hawke, *Paine*, 15

The numerous and . . . Foner, *Tom Paine and Revolutionary America*, 29

A very respectable, sensible . . . Hawke, *Paine*, 14; Fruchtman, 32

Old Greek Homer . . . Fruchtman, 32

Commodore . . . Hawke, *Paine*, 15

Who were entertained . . . Ibid., 14

His efforts won Paine . . . Fruchtman, 30; Hawke, *Paine*, 15; Foner,
    Tom Paine and Revolutionary America, 14

A record of poverty . . . Foner, *Tom Paine and Revolutionary America*, 4

Falling wages and food shortages . . . H.W. Brands, *The First American*, (New York: Anchor Books, 2002), 342–345, 404–406

In contrast to unhappy . . . Ibid., 404

Increase of money . . . Michael Foot and Isaac Kramnick, eds., *The Thomas Paine Reader*, (London: Penguin Books Ltd., 1987), 41

Ease and influence . . . Ibid., 45

Misfortune of others . . . Ibid., 41

Without such maneuvers . . . Brands, 415

. . . the King, or . . . Hawke, *Paine*, 18

The true character . . . Ibid., 17

Two of them . . . Foner, *Tom Paine and Revolutionary America*, 7–8

Years later, his finances . . . Hawke, *Paine*, 20

To make matters worse . . . Ibid., 19

He vouched for . . . Ibid., 20

Great American . . . Fruchtman, 186

3: THE CAPITAL OF THE NEW WORLD

The Regularity and Elegance . . . John Adams, Diary, August 30, 1774, in *Letters of Delegates to Congress 1774–1789*, (Provo: Folio Corp, 1992–1994), CD-ROM

At a time when . . . Mark Mayo Boatner, *Encyclopedia of the American Revolution*, (New York: David McKay Company, Inc., 1974), 856–857

It was the Quakers . . . David McCullough, *John Adams*, (New York: Simon & Schuster, 2001), 90

But the coming of . . . Foner, *Tom Paine and Revolutionary America*, 23–28, 42–44

The piece was almost . . . Hawke, *Paine*, 25

Disaffected to the . . . Philip S. Foner, ed., *The Complete Writings of Thomas Paine*, vol. II, (New York: Citadel Press, 1945), 48

I found the disposition . . . Thomas Paine, "The American Crisis VII," in *Thomas Paine: Collected Writings*, ed. Eric Foner, 194

To be sure Paine's . . . Thomas Paine, "Common Sense," in *Thomas Paine: Collected Writings*, ed. Eric Foner, 29

A wonderful talent of writing . . . Benjamin Rush, *The Autobiography of Benjamin Rush: His "Travels Through Life" together with his Commonplace Book for 1789–1813*, (Princeton: Princeton University Press, 1951), 323

Complain so loudly . . . Foner, *Tom Paine and Revolutionary America*, 73

Our subjects of conversation . . . Rush, 113

When the subject of . . . Benjamin Rush to Cheetham, 1809, in *Letters of Benjamin Rush*, ed. L.H. Butterfield, published for the American Philosophical Society, (Princeton: Princeton University Press, 1951), 1007

Hesitated . . . Rush, 114

Shuddered at the prospect . . . Rush, 114

Seized upon the idea . . . Benjamin Rush to Cheetham, 1809, in *Letters of Benjamin Rush*, ed. Butterfield, 1007

There were two words . . . David Freeman Hawke, *Benjamin Rush: Revolutionary Gadfly*, (New York: The Bobbs-Merrill Company, 1971), 137

4: A WAR OF WORDS

Beyond the ordinary short . . . Benjamin Rush to Cheetham, July, 17, 1809, in *Letters of Benjamin Rush*, ed. Butterfield, 1007

It was in pamphlets . . . Bernard Bailyn, *The Ideological Origins of the American Revolution*, (Cambridge: Belknap Press of Harvard University Press, 1992), 3

. . . responses to the great . . . Ibid., 4

Chain-reacting personal . . . Ibid., 5

Regulate the trade . . . John Dickinson, *From a Farmer in Pennsylvania to the Inhabitants of the British Colonies, Letter II*, in *Great Debates in American History*, ed. Marion Mills Miller,

(New York: Current Literature Publishing Company, 1918), 38–42

We are but parts . . . Ibid.

Some writers have . . . Thomas Paine, "Common Sense," in *Thomas Paine: Collected Writings*, ed. Eric Foner, 6

5: "A KIND OF TREASON"

Proposed giving me such . . . Thomas Paine, "The American Crisis III," in *Thomas Paine: Collected Writings*, ed. Foner, 132

Formed the outlines . . . Ibid.

Their attachment to Britain . . . Ibid., 194

English privileges have made . . . Burke speech, March 22, 1775, in *Burke's Speeches: On American Taxation, On conciliation with America and Letter to the sheriffs of Bristol*, ed. F. G. Selby, (London: MacMillan & Co., 1897)

Was prepared to deny . . . Bernard Bailyn, *The Ordeal of Thomas Hutchinson*, (Cambridge: Belknap Press of Harvard University Press, 1974), 79

. . . upon a full consideration . . . Marine Committee to Joseph Reed, March 12, 1779, in *Letters of Delegates to Congress 1774–1789*

. . . the Facts are . . . Elbridge Gerry to James Warren, July 2, 1776, in *Letters of Delegates to Congress 1774–1789*

Tolerable summary of . . . Foner, *Tom Paine and Revolutionary America*, 79

Gentlemen of the first . . . Silas Deane, August 31, 1774, in *Letters of Delegates to Congress 1774–1789*

I have Sent . . . Samuel Adams to James Warren, January 13, 1776, in *Letters of Delegates to Congress 1774–1789*

Independence was a doctrine . . . Thomas Paine, "The American Crisis III," in *Thomas Paine: Collected Writings*, ed. Foner, 130

During the fall of . . . W.E. Woodward, *George Washington: The Image and the Man*, (New York: Blue Ribbon Books, 1926), 281

There were concrete . . . McCullough, 90; Robert Middlekauff, *The Glorious Cause*, (London: Oxford University Press, 1982), 316

The Tories . . . Joseph Galloway, February 28, 1775, in *Letters of Delegates to Congress 1774–1789*

A long habit . . . Thomas Paine, "Common Sense," in *Thomas Paine: Collected Writings*, ed. Foner, 5

. . . let it be once understood . . . Burke speech, March 22, 1775, in *Burke's Speeches*, ed. F. G. Selby

[The colonists'] rights . . . Middlekauff, 318

Nothing can be . . . Thomas Paine, "Common Sense," in *Thomas Paine: Collected Writings*, ed. Foner, 22

A tolerable summary . . . Eric Foner, *Tom Paine and Revolutionary America*, 79

Like stones in a field . . . Rush, 347

Sullen tempered Pharaoh . . . Thomas Paine, "Common Sense," in *Thomas Paine: Collected Writings*, ed. Foner, 29

An ass for . . . Ibid., 16

The base remains . . . Ibid., 9–10

On whose virtue depends . . . Ibid., 9

But to understand . . . Theodore Draper, *A Struggle for Power*, (New York: Vintage, 1997), 365–367

Crowned ruffian . . . Thomas Paine, "Common Sense," in *Thomas Paine: Collected Writings*, ed. Foner, 20

A few, as a surprised . . . John Adams to James Warren, October 1775, in *Letters of Delegates to Congress 1774–1789*

Our ministerial enemies . . . Randolph Henry Lee, September 29, 1774, in *Letters of Delegates to Congress 1774–1789*

Ministerial fleet & army . . . John Sullivan to John Langdon, October 5, 1775, in *Letters of Delegates to Congress 1774–1789*

Ministerial officers . . . John Adams, June 27, 1775, in *Letters of Delegates to Congress 1774–1789*

By attacking the King . . . John C. Miller, *Origins of the American*

Revolution, (Palo Alto: Stanford University Press, 1943), 468

The wretch, that with . . . Thomas Paine, "Common Sense," in
Thomas Paine: Collected Writings, ed. Foner, 29

Ministerial Army . . . John Hancock, October 5, 1775, in Letters of
Delegates to Congress 1774–1789

King's Troops . . . Samuel Adams to Samuel Cooper, April 3, 1776,
in Letters of Delegates to Congress 1774–1789

The statue of the Royal Brute . . . William Whipple, April 11, 1776,
in Letters of Delegates to Congress 1774–1789

The history of . . . The Declaration of Independence

In all cases whatsoever . . . Pauline Maier, American Scripture, (New
York: Vintage Books, 1998), 23

Oppose not just . . . Thomas Paine, "Common Sense," in Thomas
Paine: Collected Writings, ed. Foner, 30

. . . whenever a war . . . Ibid., 25

While eating is . . . Ibid., 22

For God's sake . . . Ibid., 27

I am not induced . . . Ibid., 28

The sun never shone . . . Ibid., 21

The least fracture . . . Ibid., 21

Ye that love . . . Ibid., 36

Every spot of . . . Ibid., 36

High toned . . . Hawke, Benjamin Rush: Revolutionary Gadfly, 138

The author and printer . . . Colonel Richard Gimbel, Thomas Paine:
A Biographical Checklist of Common Sense, (New Haven: Yale
University Press, 1956), 37–39

There never was a pamphlet . . . Thomas Paine, "Forester's Letter II,"
in Thomas Paine: Collected Writings, ed. Foner, 67

6: "COMMON SENSE FOR EIGHTEEN PENCE"

I have seen . . . Samuel Adams to John Sullivan, January 12, 1776, in *Letters of Delegates to Congress 1774–1789*

Had the spirit . . . Thomas Paine, "Common Sense," in *Thomas Paine: Collected Writings*, ed. Eric Foner, 46

A piece of finished . . . Ibid.

Between January and July . . . Foner, *Tom Paine and Revolutionary America*, 119

The principles of . . . Edmund Randolph, *History of Virginia*, (Charlottesville: University Press of Virginia, 1970), 251

. . . *This morning I* . . . Josiah Bartlett to John Langdon, January 13, 1776, in *Letters of Delegates to Congress 1774–1789*

. . . *Last Evening, a Letter* . . . John Adams, April 20, 1776, in *Letters of Delegates to Congress 1774–1789*

Sir, I have only . . . Henry Wisner to John McKesson, January 13, 1776, in *Letters of Delegates to Congress 1774–1789*

The only pamphlet . . . Joseph Hewes to Samuel Johnston, February 13, 1776, in *Letters of Delegates to Congress 1774–1789*

Dear Brother . . . Samuel Ward to Henry Ward, February 19, 1776, in *Letters of Delegates to Congress 1774–1789*

The Pamphlet Common . . . Josiah Bartlett, February 19, 1776, in *Letters of Delegates to Congress 1774–1789*

It is very welcome . . . John Adams, February 19, 1776, in *The Adams Papers*, ed. L.H. Butterfield, (Cambridge: Belknap Press of Harvard University Press, 1961)

Common Sense operates . . . Oliver Wolcott to Samuel Lyman, February 3, 1776, in *Letters of Delegates to Congress 1774–1789*

. . . *Last evening* . . . John Adams to James Warren, April 20, 1774 in *Letters of Delegates to Congress 1774–1789*

The Writer of . . . John Adams to Abigail Adams, April 28, 1776, in *Letters of Delegates to Congress 1774–1789*

Imputed author . . . John Adams to Charles Lee, February 19, 1776, in *Letters of Delegates to Congress 1774–1789*

He called "Adam's Pamphlet" . . . John Rhodehamel ed., *The*

American Revolution, (New York: The Library of America, 2001), 149

So great was the triumph . . . Middlekauff, 319

There were other events . . . Boatner, 810

At a time when the . . . Foner, *Tom Paine and Revolutionary America,* 79

Paine himself felt . . . Richard M. Ketchum, *The Winter Soldiers,* (New York: Henry Holt & Company, 1975), 9

A greater run . . . Richard N. Rosenfeld, *American Aurora,* (New York: St. Martin's Press, 1997), 285

7: "INDEPENDENCE LIKE A TORRENT"

The vote being passed . . . Peterson, 12

It is well known . . . Ibid., 247

Turned Tories into Whigs . . . Foot and Kramnick, 10

You ask, what . . . John Adams, March 19, 1776, in *Letters of Delegates to Congress 1774–1789*

Evade, retard and delay . . . Thomas Flemming, *1776: Year of Illusions,* (New York: W.W. Norton & Company, 1975), 130

Postponement was the object . . . Ibid., 131

How is Common Sense . . . Fruchtman, 78

The Pamphlet called . . . William Tudor to John Adams, February, 1776, in *The Adams Papers,* ed. Butterfield

I am told by good . . . Samuel Ward, February 19, 1776, in Burnett, 137

Common Sense . . . *is read* . . . Hawke, *Paine,* 47–48

There has been a pamphlet . . . Hugh Hughes to John Adams, March 31, 1776, in *The Adams Papers,* ed. Butterfield

Seven thousand men . . . Hawke, *Benjamin Rush: Revolutionary Gadfly,* 157

Tis universally admired here . . . John Winthrop to John Adams, April 1776, in *The Adams Papers,* ed. Butterfield

People can't account . . . McCullough, 105

. . . wonder why the principles . . . James Warren to John Adams, March 7, 1776, in *The Adams Papers*, ed. Butterfield

The People are now . . . Ketchum, 15

What in the name . . . Henry Steele Commanger and Richard B. Morris eds., *The Spirit of 'Seventy Six*, (New York: Harper & Row, 1967), 283

The success of Common Sense . . . Miller, 473

They discovered that . . . Ibid.

The Author of our Miseries . . . Edmund Cody Burnett, *The Continental Congress*, (New York: The Macmillan Company, 1941), 137

Every post and . . . John Adams to James Warren, May 20, 1776, in *Letters of Delegates to Congress 1774–1789*

In South Carolina . . . Flemming, 236

The principles of Paine's . . . Randolph, 251

8: "THE DEVIL IS IN THE PEOPLE"

The Convention closed . . . Randolph, 233

A universal clamor against . . . Ibid.

Thomas Paine, an Englishman . . . Ibid.

The public sentiment . . . Ibid., 233–234

Independence, and the establishment . . . Peterson, 247

Opened to the mass . . . Ibid., 247

Common Sense *and Independence* . . . John Adams, April 20, in *Letters of Delegates to Congress 1774–1789*

My countrymen . . . Woodward, 283

. . . by private letters . . . Ibid.

One of the vilest . . . Flemming, 164

Nothing but independence . . . Ibid., 164

Whether we ought . . . Ibid., 125

Paine was not writing . . . Ibid., 124

Possessed a wonderful . . . Rush, 323

As it is my design . . . Foner, *Tom Paine and Revolutionary America*, 83

His compositions, though . . . Rush, 323

The mere independence . . . Foner, *Tom Paine and Revolutionary America*, 75

We have it in . . . Thomas Paine, "Common Sense," in *Thomas Paine: Collected Writings*, ed. Foner, 52

You have declared . . . Peter C. Messer, "Simple Argument, Plain Facts: Rethinking Thomas Paine's *Common Sense*," Rutgers University thesis

Insinuated itself into . . . Randolph, 233

. . . to have no further . . . *Independent Chronicle* (Boston), June 6, 1776

If the doctrines . . . Flemming, 128

During the suspension . . . Thomas Paine, "Rights of Man Part II," in *Thomas Paine: Collected Writings*, ed. Foner, 605

After Common Sense . . . Foner, *Tom Paine and Revolutionary America*, 75; Ketchum, 10

Minds of the people . . . John Adams to Thomas Jefferson, August 24, 1815, in *The Adams-Jefferson Letters*, ed. Lester J. Cappon, Omohunduro Institute for Early American History & Culture, (Chapel Hill: University of North Carolina Press, 1987), 455

The voice of the . . . Thomas Jefferson's Notes of Proceedings in Congress, June 7, 1776, in *Letters of Delegates to Congress 1774–1789*

Awakened the public . . . Samuel Adams to Thomas Paine, November 30, 1802, in *Thomas Paine: Collected Writings*, ed. Foner, 415

9: A PEOPLE'S ARMY

They assumed that . . . Flexner, 73

The men were . . . Ibid., 76

A dearth of . . . Ibid., 73

Within musket shot . . . Ibid., 79

The Connecticut troops . . . Commager and Morris, 162

To the inhabitants . . . Thomas Paine, "Common Sense," in *Thomas Paine: Collected Writings*, ed. Foner

Call upon the world . . . General Greene to Samuel Ward, January 4, 1776, in Commanger and Morris, 284

I have seen Common . . . John Sullivan to John Adams, March 15, 1776, in *Papers of John Adams*, ed. Robert J. Taylor, (Cambridge: Belknap Press of Harvard University Press, 1979)

Have you seen . . . General Charles Lee to George Washington, January 24, 1776, in Flexner, 73

Throughout the war . . . Benjamin Rush to Cheetham, July, 17, 1809, in *Letters of Benjamin Rush*, ed. Butterfield, 1009

They have left . . . Ketchum, 139

For The Defense . . . Flexner, 72

It Takes well with the Army . . . John Sullivan to John Adams, March 18, 1776, in *The Adams Papers*, ed. Butterfield

[He died] on . . . Royster, 101

The Congress of the year . . . Jeremiah Greenman, *Diary of a Common Soldier in the American Revolution*, (Dekalb: Northern Illinois University Press, 1978), 266

10: THE OTHER FOUNDING FATHERS

Adams knew that . . . John Adams to James Warren, April 22, 1776, in *Letters of Delegates to Congress 1774–1789*

Design of Providence . . . Ibid.

Scarcely a paper . . . John Adams to James Warren, February 14, 1776, in *Letters of Delegates to Congress 1774–1789*

That all are now united . . . John Adams to James Warren, April 22, 1776, in *Letters of Delegates to Congress 1774–1789*

As John wrote . . . John Adams to Abigail Adams, February 18, 1776, in *Letters of Delegates to Congress 1774–1789*

John Adams was a great . . . Flemming, 134

Paine was not the first . . . Maier, 99

The Great character . . . Rosenfeld, 239

Thought little of him . . . Ibid., 485

Such is the pride . . . Flexner, 63

The history of our Revolution . . . Brands, 548

Founder of the . . . Rosenfeld, 238

One gets the sense . . . Rosenfeld, 238

I am persuaded . . . Benjamin Franklin to R. Livinston, July 22,
    1783, in the Yale University Papers of Benjamin Franklin

A great deal of . . . John Adams, March 19, 1776, in *Letters of
    Delegates to Congress 1774–1789*

It has been a . . . L.H. Butterfield, ed. *Diary and Autobiography of
    John Adams*, vol II, (Cambridge: Belknap Press of Harvard
    University Press, 1962), 333

Poor, short-sighted . . . John Adams to Thomas Jefferson, June 22,
    1819, in Cappon, 542

John Adams always . . . Foner, *Tom Paine and Revolutionary America*,
    79

Worthy, ingenious young . . . Hawke, *Paine*, 20

Great effect on . . . Benjamin Franklin to the Duc de La
    Rochefoucauld, April 15, 1787, in the Yale University Papers of
    Benjamin Franklin

Be assured, my dear friend . . . Benjamin Franklin to Thomas Paine,
    September 27, 1785, in the Yale University Papers of Benjamin
    Franklin

The fondest wish . . . Flexner, 64

He wrote to his family . . . Ibid., 71

Washington, who had, . . . Ibid., 74

Sound doctrine and . . . George Washington to Joseph Reed, January
    31, 1776, in *The Writings of George Washington*, ed. Jared
    Sparks, (New York, 1848)

The General recognized . . . Don E. Ferling, *The First of Men*,
     (Knoxville: University of Tennessee Press, 1988), 158

P.S. I send you . . . Thomas Nelson to Thomas Jefferson, February 4,
     1776, in *Letters of Delegates to Congress 1774–1789*

He observed that . . . Peterson, 45

The peaceable methods . . . Thomas Paine. "Common Sense," in
     Thomas Paine: Collected Writings, ed. Foner, 45

Not being able . . . Ibid.

Laws of Nature . . . The Declaration of Independence

He has refused . . . Ibid.

Any form of . . . Ibid.

Laying its foundation . . . Ibid.

No writer has . . . Peterson, 1451

EPILOGUE: AFTER *COMMON SENSE*

Where liberty is . . . Moncure Conway, *Life of Thomas Paine*, vol. II,
     (New York: Putnam & Sons, 1893), 14

Avidity to punish . . . Thomas Paine, "Dissertation on the First
     Principles of Government," in *Complete Writings of Thomas
     Paine*, ed. Foner, 588

Day of danger . . . Ibid., 723

Crowned ruffian . . . Thomas Paine, "Common Sense," in *Complete
     Writings of Thomas Paine*, ed. Foner, 16

These are the . . . Thomas Paine, "The American Crisis," in *Thomas
     Paine: Collected Writings*, ed. Foner, 91

Must the merits . . . George Washington to James Madison, June 12,
     1784, in The George Washington Papers at the Library of
     Congress, 1741–1799

I saw, or . . . Thomas Paine, "Age of Reason I," in *Thomas Paine:
     Collected Writings*, ed. Foner, 701

BIBLIOGRAPHY

Bailyn, Bernard. *Faces of Revolution*. New York: Vintage Books, 1992.

Bailyn, Bernard. *The Ideological Origins of the American Revolution*. Cambridge: Belknap Press of Harvard University Press, 1992.

Bailyn, Bernard. *The Ordeal of Thomas Hutchinson*. Cambridge: Belknap Press of Harvard University Press, 1974.

Boatner, Mark Mayo. *Encyclopedia of the American Revolution*. New York: David McKay Company, Inc., 1974.

Brands, H.W. *The First American*. New York: Anchor Books, 2002.

Burnett, Edmund Cody. *The Continental Congress*. New York: The MacMillan Company, 1941.

Butterfield, L.H., ed. *The Adams Papers*. Cambridge: Belknap Press of Harvard University Press, 1961.

Butterfield, L.H., ed. *Diary and Autobiography of John Adams*, vol II. Cambridge: Belknap Press of Harvard University Press, 1962.

Butterfield, L.H., ed. *Letters of Benjamin Rush*. Princeton: Princeton University Press, 1951.

Cappon, Lester J., ed. *The Adams-Jefferson Letters*. Chapel Hill: University of North Carolina Press, 1987.

Commanger, Henry Steele and Richard B. Morris, eds. *Documents of American History*. New York: Appleton Century Crofts, 1968.

Conway, Moncure. *Life of Thomas Paine*, vol II. New York: Putnam & Sons, 1893.

Countryman, Edward. *The American Revolution*. New York: Hill & Wang, 1985.

Dickinson, John. *From a Farmer in Pennsylvania to Inhabitants of the British Colonies* in *Great Debates in American History*. Edited by Marion Mills Miller. New York: Current Literature Publishing Company, 1918.

Draper, Theodore. *A Struggle for Power*. New York: Vintage Books, 1997.

Ferling, John E. *The First of Men*. Knoxville: University of Tennessee Press, 1988.

Flemming, Thomas. *1776: Year of Illusions*. New York: W.W. Norton & Company, 1975.

Flexner, James Thomas. *Washington: The Indispensable Man*. Boston: Back Bay Books, 1974.

Foner, Eric. *Tom Paine and Revolutionary America*. London: Oxford University Press, 1976.

Foot, Michael, and Isaac Kramnick, eds. *The Thomas Paine Reader*. London: Penguin Books, 1987.

Fruchtman, Jack Jr. *Thomas Paine: Apostle of Freedom*. New York: Four Walls Eight Windows, 1994.

Gimbel, Colonel Richard. *Thomas Paine: A Bibliographical Checklist of Common Sense*. New Haven: Yale University Press, 1956.

Grant, Michael. *History of Rome*. New York: Charles Scribner's & Sons, 1978.

Greenman, Jeremiah. *Diary of a Common Soldier in the American Revolution*. Dekalb: Northern Illinois University Press, 1978.

Hawke, David Freeman. *Benjamin Rush: Revolutionary Gadfly*. New York: The Bobbs-Merrill Company, 1971.

Hawke, David Freeman. *Paine*. New York: W.W. Norton & Company, 1974.

Jefferson, Thomas. *Thomas Jefferson: Writings*. Edited by Merrill D. Peterson. New York: Library of America, 1984.

Ketchum, Richard M. *The Winter Soldiers*. New York: Henry Holt & Company, 1975.

Langguth, A. J. *Patriots: The Men Who Started the American Revolution*. New York: Simon and Schuster, 1991.

Larkin, Edward. "Inventing an American Public." Stanford University thesis.

Lecke, Robert. *George Washington's War*. New York: Harper Collins, 1992.

Letters of Delegates to Congress 1774–1789. CD-ROM. Provo: Folio Corp, 1992–1994.

Lunt, W.E. *History of England*. New York: Harper & Row, 1957.

Maier, Pauline. *American Scripture*. New York: Vintage Books, 1998.

Maier, Pauline. *From Resistance to Revolution*. New York: W.W. Norton, 1991.

Martin, Albert. *The War for Independence*. New York: Atheneum, 1988.

McCullough, David. *John Adams*. New York: Simon & Schuster, 2001.

Middlekauff, Robert. *The Glorious Cause*. London: Oxford University Press, 1982.

Miller, John C. *Origins of the American Revolution*. Boston: Little Brown & Company, 1943.

Peterson, Merrill D. *Thomas Jefferson: Writings*. New York: Library of America, 1984.

Paine, Thomas. *The Complete Writings of Thomas Paine*. Edited by Philip S. Foner. New York: Citadel Press, 1945.

———. *Thomas Paine: Collected Writings*. Edited by Eric Foner. New York: Library of America, 1995.

Randall, Willard Sterne. *George Washington: A Life*. New York: Henry Holt & Company, 1997.

Randolph, Edmund. *History of Virginia*. Charlottesville: University Press of Virginia, 1970.

Rhodehamel, John, ed. *The American Revolution*. New York: The Library of America, 2001.

Rosenfeld, Richard N. *American Aurora*. New York: St. Martin's Press, 1997.

Royster, Charles. *A Revolutionary People at War*. Chapel Hill: University of North Carolina Press, 1980.

Rush, Benjamin. *The Autobiography of Benjamin Rush: His "Travels Through Life" together with his Commonplace Book for 1789–1813*. Princeton: Princeton University Press, 1951.

Rush, Benjamin. *Letters of Benjamin Rush*. Edited by L. H. Butterfield. Published for the American Philosophical Society. Princeton: Princeton University Press, 1951.

Selby, F. G., ed. *Burke's Speeches: On American Taxation, On conciliation with America and Letter to the sheriffs of Bristol*. London: Macmillan & Co, 1897.

Taylor, Robert J., ed. *Papers of John Adams*. Cambridge: Belknap Press of Harvard University Press, 1979.

Washington, George Papers. The Library of Congress.

Wood, Gordon, S. *The American Revolution*. New York: Random House, 2002.

Wood, Gordon S. *Radicalism of the American Revolution*. New York: Vintage Books, 1993.

Woodward. W.E. *George Washington: The Image and the Man*. New York: Blue Ribbon Books, 1926.

INDEX